Thrilling Days in Army Life

Major George A. Forsyth, photographed at the time of the royal buffalo hunt in honor of the Russian Grand Duke Alexis in 1872. Courtesy of the National Archives, photograph 111-SC-89205.

THRILLING DAYS
✺ IN ARMY LIFE ✺
By GENERAL GEORGE A. FORSYTH, U. S. A.
WITH ILLUSTRATIONS BY RUFUS F. ZOGBAUM

Introduction to the Bison Book Edition
by David Dixon

University of Nebraska Press
Lincoln and London

Introduction to the Bison Book Edition
copyright 1994 by the University of Nebraska Press
Manufactured in the United States of America

The paper in this book meets the minimum requirements of
American National Standard for Information Sciences—Per-
manence of Paper for Printed Library Materials, ANSI
Z39.48–1984

First Bison Book printing: 1994
Most recent printing indicated by the last digit below:
10   9   8   7   6   5   4   3   2   1

Library of Congress Cataloging-in-Publication Data
Forsyth, George A.
Thrilling days in army life / by George A. Forsyth; with illus-
trations by Rufus F. Zogbaum; introduction to the Bison Book
edition by David Dixon.
p.   cm.
Originally published: New York: Harper & Brothers, 1900.
Includes bibliographical references.
ISBN 0-8032-6873-4 (pa)
1. Forsyth, George A.   2. United States—History—Civil
War, 1861–1865—Personal narratives.   3. Cedar Creek
(Va.), Battle of, 1864.   4. Appomattox Campaign, 1865.   5.
Indians of North America—Wars—1866–1895.   6. Beecher
Island, Battle of, 1868.   7. Apache Indians.   8. United
States. Army. Cavalry, 5th.   I. Title.
E601.F73   1994
973.8'092—dc20
94-18457   CIP

Reprinted from the original 1900 edition published by Harper
& Brothers, New York.

CONTENTS

ILLUSTRATIONS

INTRODUCTION

by David Dixon

Students of the frontier military are familiar with George Forsyth's name due to the soldier's heroic stand against an overwhelming number of Sioux and Cheyenne Indians at the Battle of Beecher Island in 1868. This engagement, fought in the remote expanses of eastern Colorado, embraced all of the elements of the classical epic so popular in Western cultural tradition. Newspaper editors of the day perceived the battle in terms of an age-old struggle. A savage and ruthless foe bent on overwhelming a small but courageous band; the noble leader whose fearlessness is matched only by his determination; and, the rescue in the nick-of-time which demonstrates the eventual triumph of civilization over barbarism—all were ingredients of the classical epic played out in the sand pits of Beecher Island. It is not surprising that this minor frontier skirmish was eventually transformed into a legendary symbol of sacrifice and devotion to duty in the American West. As the old veterans of the Indian Wars began to write about their experiences, few failed to mention the heroism and suffering of Forsyth and his noble band of intrepid scouts. Virtually every volume dealing with the military role in the West mentioned the battle in some detail.

Unquestionably, the most dramatic and stirring re-counting of the Beecher Island fight was written by For-syth himself. This epic tale was so compelling that later historians invariably relied on his account as their pri-mary source in providing details of the fight. Forsyth's literary success encouraged him to write other stories dealing with his long military career, and later these various articles were combined into the autobiographi-cal anthology entitled *Thrilling Days in Army Life,* originally published by Harper & Brothers in 1900.

Although this volume relates some of the most excit-ing and dramatic incidents in Forsyth's career, it does not serve as a complete biography. In fact, outside of his participation in the Beecher Island battle, few individ-uals know much about Forsyth's life. Therefore, it is ap-propriate to provide an overview of his military career.

Born in Muncy, Pennsylvania, on November 7, 1837, George Alexander Forsyth came from what he liked to call "fighting stock." He was a ninth-generation descen-dant of William Brewster who arrived in America aboard the *Mayflower.* His great-grandfather had fought in the American Revolution and had been killed in an Indian raid in 1788. Forsyth was nicknamed "Sandy" in honor of his grandfather, Alexander Forsyth, who had been wounded at the Battle of Black Rock dur-ing the War of 1812. George's uncle, John Hubbard For-syth, died alongside David Crockett and James Bowie in the defense of the Alamo.[1]

George's father, Orren, was a merchant in Muncy un-til the Panic of 1837 forced him into bankruptcy and the family relocated in Rochester, New York. Orren eventu-ally established a small manufacturing firm in the city producing scales and safes. The business thrived and he was able to send his son to a prestigious private school called Canandaigua Academy, located in the heart of western New York's "Burned-Over District, so named for the religious revivals and reform movements that swept through the area like a forest fire. Stephen A. Douglas had attended the school in preparation for a law career. Like Douglas, Forsyth himself later moved to Illinois, where he worked for a short time as a store clerk in Chicago alongside a young Marshall Field, later famous for his mercantile empire that survives to this day. Tiring of his role as a clerk and bookkeeper, Forsyth began to study law under Isaac Arnold, a leading member of the Republican party in Illinois, and a good friend of Springfield attorney Abraham Lincoln.[2]

Forsyth had just passed the bar examination when the Civil War broke out. Greatly influenced by his experiences with the abolitionist movement while in western New York, and his ties to Arnold and the Republican party, Forsyth was one of the first to enlist in Captain Charles Barker's Company of Chicago Dragoons in April 1861. After only cursory training, the company was ordered to guard the construction of river defenses at Cairo, Illinois, where the Ohio joins the Mississippi. After the gun emplacements were finished, Forsyth and the Dragoons were ordered to West Virginia as part of George B. McClellan's campaign to purge the region of Rebel forces and secure the Baltimore and Ohio Railroad. After his ninety-day enlistment expired, Forsyth returned to Chicago as a veteran campaigner.[3]

Rather than reenlist in Barker's company, Forsyth and a good friend named William Medill decided to organize an independent company to help make up a regiment of cavalry that was being raised under former Illinois congressman John Farnsworth. Medill was the younger brother of the influential editor of the *Chicago Tribune,* Joseph Medill, and the two men had little difficulty in collecting recruits. After filling the company roster, Forsyth and Medill joined the regiment, then being formed at St. Charles, Illinois. On September 18,

1861, Forsyth was enrolled as a first lieutenant in Company G, Eighth Illinois Volunteer Cavalry.[4]

Forsyth and the Eighth Illinois participated in nearly all the great campaigns of the Army of the Potomac. During the Peninsula Campaign to take Richmond in the summer of 1862, Forsyth was slightly wounded while leading a troop of cavalry on a reconnaisance patrol. Later the young lieutenant contracted malaria and was taken to an army hospital in Alexandria, Virginia. He was not able to rejoin his regiment until the fall of 1862, when he participated in the aftermath of the Battle of Antietam. Forsyth's troop was detailed to keep an eye on Robert E. Lee's retreating Confederate army.

In June 1863, Forsyth, then a captain, played an important role in the massive cavalry battle at Brandy Station, where he was severely wounded in the right thigh. The young officer did not recuperate from this wound until the winter of 1863, thereby missing the Battle of Gettysburg. The one bright moment during this grueling period came when Forsyth received word of his promotion to major.

In the spring of 1864, while the Eighth Illinois was serving on routine guard duty around the nation's capital, Forsyth asked officials in the War Department for an independent combat command. His request was granted and Major Forsyth formed a cavalry regiment of convalescents and unassigned veterans. This unit provided valuable reconnaissance information to General Grant's forces during the Wilderness campaign. Forsyth's abilities were noticed by the fiery cavalry commander, Philip H. Sheridan, who asked the major to join his staff as an aide, thus beginning a relationship that would last for nearly twenty years.[5]

Throughout the final bloody months of the Civil War, Forsyth gained an enviable reputation as one of the most energetic and courageous officers in the Union

Cavalry. At the Battle of Winchester, General James Harrison Wilson recalled Forsyth galloping up, exclaiming, "This is splendid; you have got a bully fight on hand!" Wilson wrote, "Then waving his hat, he dashed into the thick of it. . . ."[6] One time a reporter asked Michael Sheridan, the general's brother and another staff officer, what it felt like to be under fire for the first time. Sheridan replied, "I recollect that I wished I were somewhere else, a feeling that was experienced by all the soldiers I knew except Major George Forsyth. Forsyth was ready any time to risk his life, even though it was not actually necessary, and seemed to take joy in entering a fight."[7]

An aide to the flamboyant Sheridan, Forsyth was on the scene during some of the most dramatic episodes of the Civil War. He was with Sheridan on the famous ride from Winchester to Cedar Creek and provided history with the most thorough account of that legendary event. Forsyth was also present when Union forces dealt the final death blow to Robert E. Lee's once powerful Army of Northern Virginia.

Following the end of the war, Major Forsyth received a commission in the regular army and was assigned to Sheridan's staff as inspector general. After serving over two years in Louisiana during Reconstruction, Sheridan was transferred to the West, where he assumed command of the Department of the Missouri in 1868. Forsyth accompanied his chief as an aide.

Duties in the vast department centered on curtailing the activities of Plains Indians who were resisting the steady encroachment of whites and the construction of the railroads. The wave of Indian raids in the Solomon and Saline valleys in Kansas in the late summer of 1868 set in motion the chain of events that would bring near-death and lasting fame to George Forsyth in the sand pits known as Beecher Island.

During the first day of the battle Forsyth was shot three times: in the right thigh, left leg, and head, the last where a Henry rifle ball removed a quarter size piece of his skull.[8] Despite these severe injuries, Forsyth retained at least nominal command throughout the nine-day siege. When Captain Louis Carpenter's detachment of the Tenth Cavalry arrived to relieve the beleaguered company of scouts, the captain noticed that the desperately wounded major "affected to be reading an old novel" in order to keep from breaking down.[9] Forsyth and the other wounded men were removed from the island and taken to a nearby plum thicket to receive medical attention. Dr. Jenkins A. Fitzgerald believed that Forsyth's left leg was so badly infected that amputation was required. The major refused to part with his limb, and the doctor dressed his wounds and transported him to Fort Wallace, Kansas, with the other injured scouts. Bone fragments making up nearly three inches of the left tibia were removed, and physicians at the post hospital were fearful that Forsyth would never walk again. Surprisingly, cartilage filled in the gap where the bone had been removed and, after nearly a year, Forsyth was finally able to walk without the aid of crutches.

After recovering from his wounds, Forsyth returned to duty on Sheridan's staff. The general, then commanding the much larger Military Division of the Missouri, made his headquarters in Chicago. While the division commander was tied to headquarters with administrative duties, he detailed Forsyth to make various inspections throughout his command. In 1872 Forsyth went to Utah to investigate the possibility of a Mormon uprising. The following year he made the first steamboat reconnaissance up the Yellowstone River. In 1874 the loyal staff officer served as Sheridan's personal representative on George Custer's Black Hills Expedition.

From 1875 to early 1877, Forsyth accompanied General Emory Upton on a tour around the world to view the armies of Asia and Europe and make recommendations for American army reform.[10]

In 1881 Forsyth was promoted to lieutenant colonel and ordered to join his new regiment, the Fourth Cavalry, in New Mexico. For the next five years Forsyth participated in the final phases of the Apache wars in the Southwest. One grueling pursuit of noted Apache leaders Loco, Juh, and Geronimo led Forsyth across the border into Mexico in 1882. His reminiscences of this campaign are included in this volume.[11]

In 1888 Forsyth was court-martialed for duplicating his own pay vouchers to satisfy various creditors. The colonel had for some years been obsessed with speculating in the commodities and stock markets, and the compulsion had turned into an illness. Found guilty, Forsyth was sentenced to be dismissed from the service. Only by direct intervention from President Grover Cleveland was the sentence reduced to suspension for a period of three years. Forsyth returned home to Chicago, where further investigation into his financial improprieties determined that his behavior was a direct result of the gunshot wound to the head that he had received at the Battle of Beecher Island. Consequently, Forsyth's sentence was remitted: he was restored to rank but forced to retire from the military in 1890. After nearly twenty-nine years of active duty, eighteen full-scale battles, forty skirmishes, six battlefield wounds, five brevet commissions and countless reconnaissance and inspection tours, George Forsyth was finally out of the army.[12]

Following his retirement, Forsyth moved to Washington in order to lobby personally the War Department in an attempt to be restored to active duty. As his chances of returning to the military dwindled, it was only natural for the old soldier to reflect on his long and distinguished career. After poring over his old reports and other official documents in the War Department, Forsyth sat down to write his own version of the Beecher Island fight. Previously, other army officers such as George Custer, James B. Fry, and General Sheridan had written about the engagement; but only Forsyth could provide the stirring details and sense of realism that could come only from one who was there.[13]

Students of the battle recognize that Forsyth's account of the action is somewhat embellished. For example, in his version of the fight Forsyth claims that the Chief Guide, Abner Grover, recognized the Northern Cheyenne war leader, Roman Nose. On the contrary, no contemporary account mentioned the famous Indian by name. However, an article in the *New York Herald* written shortly after the battle mentioned that the Indians were exhorted by a chief "with the claws of birds and animals, the coronet of feathers and the eagle beak upon his head." This description closely resembles the war bonnet worn by Roman Nose during the battle.[14] Despite this obvious embellishment for the sake of drama, Forsyth's narrative of events is fairly accurate and substantiated by contemporary accounts and the reminiscences of the other scouts.[15]

After completing his manuscript, Forsyth submitted the article to *Harper's New Monthly Magazine,* one of the most popular journals of the day. The illustrated magazine contained articles dealing with science, popular history, and literature from renowned authors such as Mark Twain and Woodrow Wilson. Forsyth's manuscript, simply titled "A Frontier Fight," was accepted for publication and appeared in the June 1895 issue. Forsyth received $350 for his efforts.[16]

Forsyth's tale of noble sacrifice and the eventual triumph of civilization over barbarism came at a time when America was on the verge of spreading Anglo-Saxon civilization around the globe to "inferior peoples." "A Frontier Fight" seemed to reinforce the concept of Social Darwinism that fueled imperialistic tendencies, and the article was an immediate success. Forsyth received letters of praise and congratulation from across the country. One admirer wrote to him stating that she "trembled, shuddered, agonized, laughed and wept over it."[17] A review, which appeared in the *Woodland [California] Daily Democrat,* stated that the story was "well written in the simplest and most forcible language. It deserved a place of honor in our school readers and works of relocution [*sic*]. Never have I been so impressed by a piece of literature."[18]

Following the success of "A Frontier Fight," Forsyth wrote "Sheridan's Ride," which appeared in the July 1897 issue of *Harper's.* The poem of the same name by Thomas Buchanan Read had, by this time, become common recitation for school children who were familiar with General Sheridan's dramatic gallop up the Shenandoah Valley in 1864 to reach his shattered command. The general's arrival on the battlefield at Cedar Creek revitalized his stunned troops and turned defeat into victory.[19] To insure historical accuracy, Forsyth went over the area with military artist Rufus Zogbaum, who was commissioned to illustrate the article.[20]

In writing the story Forsyth again took some poetic license by sanitizing Sheridan's language in rallying his men to return to the battlefield. As Forsyth recalled, "To the best of my recollection, from the time we met the first stragglers who had drifted back from the army, his appearance and his cheery shout of 'Turn back, men! turn back! Face the other way!' as he waved his hat towards the front, had but one result: a wild cheer of recognition, an answering wave of the cap."[21] Army surgeon C. H. Parry also witnessed Sheridan's ride that

morning but remembered the general's language somewhat differently. As Parry recalled, Sheridan reined in
his mount and admonished the stragglers saying, "God
damn you, don't cheer me! If you love your country, come
up to the front! There's lots of fight in you men yet! Come
up, God damn you! Come up!"[22]

Forsyth also contributed an article to *Harper's* dealing with the final days of the Civil War. The trusty aide
was one of the few fortunate men to be present at Appomattox Court House when Lee surrendered his once
invincible army to General Grant. Forsyth sat on the
porch of the McLean House while the surrender terms
were being discussed in the parlor.

George Forsyth's last literary contribution to *Harper's* related his experiences during an Apache campaign in the Southwest. Contrary to orders, Forsyth,
with six troops of cavalry and a contingent of Indian
scouts, crossed the Mexican border in pursuit of a band
of Apaches that had bolted from the San Carlos Agency
in Arizona in 1882. The fleeing Apaches were so preoc-
cupied with the American troops in their rear that they
inadvertently walked into an ambush set by Mexican
soldiers. Later some Arizona frontiersmen and pioneers
criticized the colonel's actions during the campaign; but
generals Sheridan, Sherman, and Pope sent letters of
congratulation to Forsyth for his dogged pursuit.[23] The
article, "An Apache Raid," was published in the January
14, 1899, issue of *Harper's Weekly*.

A year after the publication of "An Apache Raid,"
Harper & Brothers proposed that all of Forsyth's previous articles be collected into book form and published
as an anthology entitled *Thrilling Days in Army Life*.
The agreement Forsyth signed with the publisher provided him with ten percent royalties on the trade list
price of $2.00 per copy for the first two thousand copies
sold. Thereafter, the old soldier was to receive a fifteen
percent royalty.[24]

Forsyth's literary career did not end with the publication of *Thrilling Days in Army Life*. He also contributed to D. Appleton's "Story of the West" series: *The Story of the Soldier* was published in 1900. Like *Thrilling Days in Army Life,* this volume was well received. The book review editor of the *New York Times* said, "Gen. Forsyth's narrative contains the most melancholy recitals of Indian atrocities, so that as one reads he realizes the grim truth of the statement that the only good Indian is a dead one, and so the story goes."[25]

In his final years of retirement George Forsyth kept up a lively correspondence and dabbled in genealogy. He returned to the West once in 1905 to attend a reunion of the old scouts who had fought at the Battle of Beecher Island. He always maintained strong bonds of affection for these grizzled veterans, proclaiming them to be "wonderfully good men."[26] The scouts held Forsyth in high regard as well. In a letter to the colonel written in anticipation of the 1905 reunion, former scout Jack Peate remarked, "The boys think a great deal of their old commander."[27] By this time, the infirm soldier was forced to walk with two canes due to the debilitating affects of his old war wounds. Nonetheless, he made his way to the speaker's platform at Beecher Island and gave a rousing speech to the assembled veterans and other guests.

George Forsyth spent the remainder of his life at his home in Rockport, Massachusetts, with his wife Natalie Sedgewick Beaumont Forsyth. He died from heart disease on September 12, 1915, and is buried in Arlington National Cemetery.

Despite the passage of nearly a century, *Thrilling Days in Army Life* still makes for exciting reading. Although Forsyth wrote in a somewhat stiff, Victorian style, his prose can still conjure up compelling images of combat and human drama. Modern readers will find some of the depictions of Indian life and culture to be offensive; yet Forsyth's language reveals the prevailing attitudes of the period. Long out of print and becoming increasingly difficult to locate, *Thrilling Days in Army Life* has become a classic in the literature of the frontier military, and students of the period will find this reprint edition to be a welcome addition to their collections.

NOTES

1. Forsyth Genealogical Papers, courtesy of Mabel Baxter, Briggsdale, Colorado. Much of the information contained in this collection was gathered by Forsyth himself.

2. Charles F. Milliken, *A History of Ontario County, New York, and Its People,* 2 vols. (New York: Lewis Historical Publishing Company, 1911), 1:266–309; "Brig. Gen. G. A. Forsyth: A First-Class Fighting Man," *Washington Herald,* March 17, 1907, newspaper clipping in George A. Forsyth Papers, Colorado Historical Society, Denver, Colorado.

3. George A. Forsyth, Military Record, in George A. Forsyth, Appointment, Commission, Personal File, Records of the Adjutant General, Record Group 94, File # 4874ACP1881, Military Service Branch, National Archives, Washington, D.C. [hereafter cited as Forsyth ACP File]. Information relative to Charles Barker's Chicago Dragoons can be found in the *Chicago Tribune,* January 24, 1861; April 19, 1861; August 1, 5, 6, 1861.

4. Information regarding the Eighth Illinois Volunteer Cavalry can be found in Abner Hard, *History of the Eighth Cavalry Regiment, Illinois Volunteers* (Aurora, Illinois: Privately Printed, 1868; reprint, Dayton: Morningside Bookshop, 1984).

5. George A. Forsyth, Military Record, in Forsyth ACP File.

6. James Harrison Wilson, *Under the Old Flag,* 2 vols. (New York: D. Appleton, 1912), 1:552–53.

7. James B. Morrow, "Story of Sheridan's Ride Told by Sheridan's Brother," *Boston Globe,* December 11, 1910, newspaper clipping in Forsyth Papers.

8. Information about the extent of Forsyth's wounds can be found in Proceedings of a Board of Medical Officers concerning the mental condition of Lt. Col. George A. Forsyth, December 1, 1896, in Forsyth ACP File.

9. See p. 73, this book. The best account of the rescue of Forsyth's command can be found in MerryLu Simmons and Robert Simmons, eds., *The Beecher Island Annual* (Wray, Colorado: Beecher Island Battle Memorial Association, 1985), 64–67, 98–100.

10. Forsyth's official reports on various military excursions can be found in the Philip H. Sheridan Papers, Library of Congress, Washington, D.C.

11. Aside from Forsyth's own recollections of this campaign, readers should consult Papers Relating to Outbreaks of Indians at San Carlos, Arizona Territory, Records of the Adjutant General, Record Group 94, Doc. File # 1749AGO1882, Military Service Branch, National Archives, Washington, D.C.; and Record of Events, kept by John B. Guthrie of Forsyth's Expedition against the Apaches, April, 1882, Order of the Indian Wars Papers, File X-18, U.S. Army Military History Institute, Carlisle Barracks, Pennsylvania.

12. Information regarding Forsyth's court-martial can be found in Proceedings in the Case of Lt. Col. George A. Forsyth, Fourth Cavalry, Fort Huachuca, Arizona Territory, 1888, Records of the Judge Advocate General, Record Group 153, Military Service Branch, National Archives, Washington, D.C.

13. For accounts of the Beecher Island fight written before Forsyth's own published version, readers should consult George A. Custer, *My Life on the Plains* (New York: Shelden and Company, 1874); James B. Fry, *Army Sacrifices; or Briefs from Official Pigeon-Holes* (New York: D. Van Norstrand, 1879); P. H. Sheridan, *Personal Memoirs of P. H. Sheridan,* 2 vols. (New York: Charles Webster, 1888); and De B. Randolph Keim, *Sheridan's Troopers on the Borders* (Philadelphia: Claxton, Remsen and Haffelfinger, 1870).

14. Perhaps the best contemporary account of the battle was written by *New York Herald* correspondent De B. Randolph Keim, who interviewed the scouts immediately following their return to Fort Wallace, Kansas. This account can be found in the *New York Herald,* October 12, 1868.

15. Another obvious error made by Forsyth in writing his account of the engagement is his description of much of the action taking place from east to west. When he traveled to the

battlefield in 1905 for a reunion with his scouts, he recognized his mistake and commented that he should have visited the site before writing his story.

16. In Forsyth's Medical Board Proceedings, his wife, Natalie Sedgewick Beaumont Forsyth, commented that her husband received $350 for each article published in *Harper's*.

17. Edith Bromer to George A. Forsyth, July 31, 1895, in William L. Lance Collection, Arizona Historical Society, Tucson, Arizona.

18. Undated clipping from the *Woodland Daily Democrat*, in Forsyth Papers.

19. For information on the Battle of Cedar Creek, readers should consult Jeffery D. Wert, *From Winchester to Cedar Creek: The Shenandoah Campaign of 1864* (Carlisle, Pennsylvania: South Mountain Press, 1987).

20. R. F. Zogbaum to George A. Forsyth, May 30, 1895, in William L. Lance Collection, Arizona Historical Society, Tucson, Arizona.

21. Forsyth, *Thrilling Days in Army Life,* 141.

22. Sheridan's oath, recorded by Surgeon Parry, can be found in Stephen Z. Starr, *The Union Cavalry in the Civil War,* 3 vols. (Baton Rouge: Louisiana State University Press, 1979–1985), 2:312.

23. Criticism concerning Forsyth's activities during this Apache campaign can be found in Dan Thrapp, *Al Sieber: Chief of Scouts* (Norman: University of Oklahoma Press, 1964), 223; Dan Thrapp, *General George Crook and the Sierra Madre Adventure* (Norman: University of Oklahoma Press, 1972), 61; and, Hoyt Sanford Vandenberg, Jr., "Forsyth and the 1882 Loco Outbreak Campaign," *The Smoke Signal* (Tucson: Tucson Corral of Westerners, 1993), 174–96.

24. Harper & Brothers to George A. Forsyth, February 27, 1900, in Forsyth Papers.

25. *New York Times,* February 2, 1901.

26. Forsyth, *The Story of the Soldier* (New York: D. Appleton and Company, 1900), 212.

27. J. J. Peate to George A. Forsyth, July 28, 1905, in Forsyth Papers.

A FRONTIER FIGHT

[p. 138

TO THE FRONT FROM WINCHESTER

A FRONTIER FIGHT

MORE than twenty-five years agone it so fell out that I was an actor in one of the most important Indian campaigns of the last half of the present century—the second of a series of four such campaigns, all fought since our civil war, that finally broke down the power of the various semi-united tribes, compelled them to accept the reservation system, and has practically ended savage warfare within the present limits of the United States.

Not that I regard the Indian question as settled, for we still have to face some knotty problems regarding the final disposition of the red men, and it is not at all improbable that within the next decade there will be more or less fighting of a sanguinary character until eventually a fixed policy regarding the Indians will be evolved, and their gradual absorption into the body politic will take place. It is the story in detail of one of the frontier fights that occurred during the second of the four campaigns above mentioned that I now propose to tell. In the summer of 1868 I was on duty as

3

acting inspector-general of the Department of the Missouri, serving in that capacity upon the staff of General Philip H. Sheridan, who was then in command of that military department, with headquarters at Fort Leavenworth, Kansas. The geographical limits of the department included the States of Missouri, Arkansas, and Kansas, and the three territories of Colorado, New Mexico, and Indian Territory. Incidentally, the campaign of which I write carried us somewhat beyond the above-named limits on the north, and into northern Texas on the south. However, within the boundaries I have named, many of the tribes who at that time were either openly or covertly hostile to the government had their hunting grounds, and roamed at will over the plains and along the frontier from northwestern Texas on the south to the British possessions on the north, having for their habitat all of the then unsettled country east of the Rocky Mountains. In those days it was an Indian paradise, for within a few miles of the most advanced settlements, plover, quail, and grouse sprang into the air with a startled whirr, and fluttered away to cover in every direction, as the early traveller urged his horse along the trail or through the thick grass that bordered the path on his journey's way. Wild fowl of almost every variety nested and raised their young fearlessly in the reeds along the course of the rivers and among the lakes and swamps of the South and West, while vast flocks of wild turkeys feasted and fattened on the hazel and pecan-nuts of Indian Territory and Texas. The mountain streams were filled with trout, and far in the rugged depths of the Rocky Mountains brown, black, and grizzly bear, together with wild-cat and mountain-lion, gave the added zest of danger to the Indian hunters; bands of elk and antelope and herds of deer ranged at will along the streams and among the foot-hills of the mountains, while the great plains were at times covered as far as the eye could reach with vast herds of buffalo, which grazed, comparatively unmolested, from Indian Territory on the south to the bad lands of Dakota on the north. During our great civil war, from 1861 to 1865, the western and southwestern frontier had in many places receded. The Indians had become possessed of fire-arms, in some cases of the most modern invention, and, with their warlike instincts, were quick to learn their use, and prompt to apply it in action, and in the absence of government troops had pressed back the advancing lines of settlements, harried the weaker hamlets, killed the scattered frontiersmen, outraged and murdered their women, and carried their younger children into captivity.

A FRONTIER FIGHT

Upon the reoccupation of the southern and western frontier by government troops at the close of the war, the Indians, who had grown confident in their own strength, were greatly exasperated, and the construction of the Union Pacific Railroad across the continent to the Pacific coast, directly through their hunting-grounds, drove them almost to frenzy. The spring of 1868 found them arrogant, defiant, and confident, and late in the summer of that year they boldly threw off all concealment, abrogated their treaties, and entered upon the war-path. I have lying before me, as I write, a tabulated statement of the outrages committed by the Indians within the Military Department of the Missouri from June until December of that year, and it shows one hundred and fifty-four murders of white settlers and freighters, and the capture of numerous women and children, the burning and sacking of farm-houses, ranches, and stage-coaches, and gives details of horror and outrage visited upon the women that are better imagined than described.

For at least two years prior to the time of this general outbreak much trouble had existed between the Indians and the settlers. Murders of settlers by detached war parties of Indians, reprisals by the settlers, and engagements between the Indians and soldiers, with varying successes and defeats on both sides, had developed bad blood, and no small amount of hatred, between the whites and the aborigines. At this late day it is useless to discuss the causes that led to this state of affairs; that there were faults in abundance on both sides there is little or no doubt, but taken in its entirety, it was the advance of civilization against barbarism, with the assurance in the end of "the survival of the fittest," a harsh, cruel, but seemingly inexorable, law, that has obtained since the dawn of creation. My experience of military life having been gained solely in our civil war, the only fairly accurate knowledge I had of Indians had been picked up during a year's service in the Department of the Missouri, as I travelled through its limits on duty as inspector, and notwithstanding I had assimilated, or tried to, all that I had seen or heard regarding them, my knowledge was most meagre. It might have been summed up under three heads. First, that they were shrewd, crafty, treacherous, and brave. Secondly, that they were able warriors in that they took no unnecessary risks, attacked generally from ambush, and never in the open field unless in overwhelming numbers. Thirdly, that they were savages in all that the word implies, gave no quarter, and defeat at their hands meant annihilation, either in the field, or by torture at the stake,

7

A FRONTIER FIGHT

As soon as it became evident that war was the only alternative on the part of the government, I made up my mind to try for a command in the field. The regiment to which I belonged was serving in another department; as a major in the line, I was conspicuously a junior. To displace any one of my seniors for the purpose of giving me a command in the field would have been rank favoritism, a thing not to be thought of by the commanding general or myself. Still, I could not give up the idea of an active command. After several days' cogitation I went to General Sheridan, told him that I thought I could do better service both for him and the government in the coming campaign if I had an active command than I could possibly render as a staff-officer, that I did not see how he could provide me with a command of any kind under the existing condition of affairs, but I wished that, in case opportunity offered, he would kindly consider my request for the first field vacancy.

General Sheridan listened quietly to what I had to say, and then replied in substance as follows: "I have seen for some time what has been on your mind, and if you were senior to certain of the officers about to take the field, I would find other duty for them and give you a command, but as you are junior to them, I cannot consistently do so. There will be, however, an opportunity for you in a small way, if you care to take it. It is a command that is not at all commensurate with your rank or reputation, but it is all I have. Understand, if you decline it, I shall have no feeling whatever in the matter." "What is it?" was my query. "I have determined to organize a scouting party of fifty men from among the frontiersmen living here on the border. There is no law that will permit me to enlist them, and I can only employ them as scouts through the quartermaster's department. I will offer them a dollar a day, and thirty-five cents a day for the use of their horses, which will, I think, bring good material. Of course the government will equip them, and they will draw soldiers' rations. If you care for the command, you can have it, and I will give you Lieutenant Fred Beecher, of the Third Infantry, for your second in command." " Thank you, general," was my response, " and I could not ask a better lieutenant than Beecher. I accept the command with pleasure." "I thought you would, and yet I hesitated to offer it. Understand, if I had anything better, you should have it." " I am glad to get this," was my reply.

An hour later I was handed the following order:

HEADQUARTERS DEPARTMENT OF THE MISSOURI,
FORT HARKER, *August 24,* 1868.
Brevet Colonel George A. Forsyth, A. A. Inspector-General,
Department of the Missouri.
COLONEL,—The general commanding directs that you,

without delay, employ fifty (50) first-class hardy frontiersmen, to be used as scouts against the hostile Indians, to be
commanded by yourself, with Lieutenant Beecher, Third
Infantry, as your subordinate. You can enter into such
articles of agreement with these men as will compel obedience.

I am, sir, very respectfully,
Your obedient servant,
(Sgd.) J. SCHUYLER CROSBY,
A. D. C. & A. A. Adjutant-General.

In the year I write of there was little trouble
in obtaining capable and competent men for
my new command. Hundreds of men who had
served through the bitter civil strife of 1861 to
1865, either for or against the government, had
flocked to the frontier, and were willing, and even
anxious, to assist in punishing the Indians, while
many a frontiersman was only too glad to have
an opportunity to settle an old score against the
savages. In two days I had enrolled thirty men
at Fort Harker, and marching from there to Fort
Hayes, sixty miles westward, I completed my
complement in two days more, and on the 20th
of August, five days from the time I had received
the order, we took the field.

The only difficulty I experienced was in mounting my men, some of whom had no horses, and
were too poor to buy them; but this trouble was
obviated by certain frontiersmen, notably Dick
Parr (an interpreter and scout at General Sheridan's headquarters), who furnished the men sev-

eral of his own horses, and persuaded other frontiersmen to do the same thing, they agreeing to take the thirty-five cents a day (which I was authorized to offer, through the quartermaster's department of the army) for their use, and in case of their loss on the march, or in action, they were to be paid their full value.

Our equipment was simple: A blanket apiece, saddle and bridle, a lariat and picket-pin, a canteen, a haversack, butcher-knife, tin plate and tin cup. A Spencer repeating rifle (carrying six shots in the magazine, besides the one in the barrel), a Colt's revolver, army size, and 140 rounds of rifle and 30 rounds of revolver ammunition per man—this carried on the person. In addition, we had a pack-train of four mules, carrying camp-kettles and picks and shovels, in case it became necessary to dig for water, together with 4000 extra rounds of ammunition, some medical supplies, and extra rations of salt and coffee. Each man, officers included, carried seven days' cooked rations in his haversack.

It was no ordinary command, this company of fifty scouts, and I have little doubt but that each and every trooper, both young and old, had a history worth hearing, if he had cared to tell it.

As of late years there has been some discussion as to who were the men who were with me in the fight on the Arickaree Fork of the Republican

River, I herewith append the list, as copied from the original roll. All but four of these men were native Americans, and a number of them college graduates, and I never saw but one company of enlisted men who I thought exceeded them in general intelligence: First Lieutenant Fred. H. Beecher, Third Infantry, U. S. Army; Acting Assistant Surgeon J. H. Mooers, Medical Department, U. S. A.; Abner T. Grover, chief scout; Wm. H. H. McCall, first sergeant; W. Armstrong, Thos. Alderdice, Martin Burke, Wallace Bennett, G. W. Chalmers, G. B. Clarke, John Donovan, Bernard Day, Alfred Dupont, A. J. Entler, Louis Farley, Hudson Farley, Richard Gantt, George Green, John Haley, John Hurst, Frank Harrington, J. H. Ketterer, John Lyden, M. R. Lane, Joseph Lane, C. B. Nichols, George Oakes, M. R. Mapes, Thomas Murphy, Howard Morton, H. T. McGrath, Thomas O'Donnell, C. C. Piatt, A. J. Pliley, William Reilly, Thomas Ranahan, Chalmers Smith, J. S. Stillwell, S. Schlesinger, Edward Simpson, William Stewart, H. H. Tucker, Isaac Thayer, Pierre Truedeau, Fletcher Violett, William Wilson, C. B. Whitney, John Wilson, Eli Ziegler, Louis McLaughlin, Harry Davenport, T. K. Davis.

My lieutenant, Fred. H. Beecher, of the Third U. S. Infantry, was a most lovable character. He was the son of the Rev. Charles Beecher, brother of Henry Ward Beecher, the distinguished divine.*

My acquaintance with him had begun in a peculiar manner, and now that so many years have intervened since his death, I think I can venture to put upon paper a matter that thoroughly exhibits the manly character he was, and that may possibly help some other youngster to call a halt when he first realizes that his appetite for liquor is getting the better of him. I had heard much of Lieutenant Beecher as one of the most promising young officers in the army, and had conceived a strong liking for the man, but had never yet met him. One day, early in the spring of 1868, when accidentally present at a consultation where General Sheridan was determining a plan of action, his name was mentioned as a man likely to exactly fill the requirements of a certain delicate mission to one of the disaffected tribes, and the order detailing him was about to be made when an elderly officer spoke up and said that within a few months Lieutenant

---

*He served through the civil war with great gallantry, and was lamed for life with a bullet through his knee at the battle of Gettysburg. Energetic, active, reliable, brave, and modest, with a love of hunting and a natural taste for plainscraft, he was a splendid specimen of a thoroughbred American, and a most valuable man in any position requiring coolness, courage, and tact, and especially so for the campaign we were about entering upon.

Beecher had become habituated to a daily use of liquor that, in his judgment, might possibly render such a detail, under the peculiar circumstances governing the case, a little hazardous. This statement resulted in the order for the detail being temporarily suspended. I saw that General Sheridan looked surprised and disappointed, and I certainly felt so myself. After thinking the matter over for a few hours, I sat down and wrote Lieutenant Beecher a letter. I stated that, as I only knew him by reputation, he might, and probably would, be surprised at the tenor of my communication, but that having conceived a strong liking for him, from what I knew of his record, I wished that he would look upon my letter as written solely in his own best interest, and that I was penning it without a thought of official position in any way. I then tersely told him how he had lost an opportunity for possible distinction owing to the fact that it was feared that he had contracted too great a fondness for liquor. I gave him no names, but assured him that the statement regarding his newly formed habit came from an officer of years and rank, who could have had no possible personal feeling in the matter, and earnestly adjured him to give it up, as it was unquestionably injuring his reputation. In closing, I admitted that I had lain myself open to criticism and possible animadversion upon his part, but that I had done by him as I would that any one in a similar position would have done by a younger brother of my own under the same circumstances, and I begged to be allowed to subscribe myself, though personally unknown to him, his sincere friend and well-wisher. It was some days before I received an answer, and I began to doubt somewhat the wisdom of my course. When the answer finally came, however, I doubted no longer. Of all the manly letters! I wish I could recall it word for word, but I can only give from memory the concluding sentence: "From to-day John Barleycorn and I part company forever." It was the truth; never again to the day of his death did Fred Beecher put a glass of whiskey to his lips. I took the letter to General Sheridan, who was greatly pleased, both with Beecher's letter and my action, and the suspended detail was promptly made. When I first met him, a few months later, at Fort Wallace, some weeks prior to the Indian outbreak, I need scarcely say we met as friends, and the better I grew to know him the more I admired and liked him. Of the younger men I knew, none would have been more acceptable to me as a second in command.

My guide was Sharp Grover, a plainsman of somewhere between forty and fifty years of age, who had passed his life in hunting and trapping along the northwestern border. About five feet ten inches in height, rather sparely built, little given to conversation, and apt to be somewhat moody at times, and, as I grew to know him better, I judged from his manner and his swarthy complexion that he had in his blood a dash of the French voyageur, probably from among his mother's people. He was well posted in Indian craft, spoke the dialect of the Sioux, and knew many of their tribe personally. A keen eye, a good shot, and a cool head made him a valuable man. He had just recovered from a wound in the back, received while leaving Turkey Legs Camp, on the Solomon River, where he and Mr. William Comstock had been sent to ascertain the truth of the rumor that the Sioux were about to go upon the war-path. The Indians professed friendship, but at the same time insisted upon Comstock and Grover leaving the camp. Seven Indians went with them, ostensibly friendly, but, while conversing with them, fell slightly to the rear on the trail and suddenly opened fire upon them, shooting them both in the back. Comstock was killed instantly, but Grover, though badly wounded, threw himself on the ground, and from behind the dead body of his friend opened on them with his repeating rifle, drove them back, and as it was late in the day, kept them off until dark, and finally escaped during the night. Comstock, at the time of his death, was regarded as the most capable and reliable scout in the government service. He, Dick Parr, Sharp Grover, and William Cody (Buffalo Bill) were, at the time I write of, 1868, a strong quartet of able and competent plainsmen, bred to their work by years of service, and men to be relied upon under all circumstances. As my scouts were to serve as soldiers, I organized the command as a troop of cavalry. My first sergeant was a man of about thirty years of age, who had served throughout the civil war with more than ordinary distinction. He was General William H. H. McCall, had been colonel of a Pennsylvania regiment, and had been brevetted a brigadier-general for his brilliant services at the time General J. B. Gordon, of the Confederate forces, early one morning in the spring of 1865, during the siege of Petersburg, assaulted and carried Fort Stedman. Scarcely had the gallant Confederate gained the works, when McCall picked up his regiment, which lay along the line of investment, and dashed into the fort, and after a desperate struggle, in which great bravery was shown on both sides, succeeded in driving out the enemy and capturing a number of prisoners, reoccupying the works with our forces. McCall, like many another good man of either army,

had drifted West since the close of the war, been
unsuccessful, became a bit dissipated, and just
at this period was ready and willing to take the
chances in anything that offered an opportunity
for advancement or distinction. Martin Burke,
one of the privates, an Irishman, had served in
the English army in India with the Sixty-fourth
of the line (Second Staffordshire), and also the
Thirty-first, from which he was invalided owing
to sunstroke, sent home to England and pen-
sioned, came to America in 1861, enlisted in a
New York volunteer regiment, served through
the civil war, was transferred to the Third United
States Cavalry, and when I met and enrolled
him had just been honorably discharged, with
the grade of corporal. He was a splendid soldier,
and proved himself a man among men in the
darkest hours we saw during our short campaign,
and throughout the civil war. Of the others,
to the best of my recollection, Bennett, Clarke,
Donovan, Dupont, Green, Haley, Hurst, Harrington, Ketterer, Joe Lane, Oakes, Murphy,
Piatt, Pliley, Chalmers Smith, Simpson, Stewart, Thayer, Whitney, Ziegler, McLaughlin,
and Davenport had served in either the regular
army or the United States or Confederate volunteers. The two best shots of our troop were Louis
Farley and his young son, Hudson Farley, both
frontiersmen, and, I think, farmers by occupa-

tion, men of great coolness and unsurpassed bravery. Taken all in all, it was rather a remarkable aggregation, considering how hurriedly it was picked up and thrown forward instantly into the field. For the first few days there was some friction, naturally enough; then discipline told, and the men got down to their work, and there was no further trouble. Early on the morning of the 29th of August, 1868, I received the following at the hands of the Acting Adjutant-General, Colonel J. Schuyler Crosby:

FORT HAYS, KANSAS, *August 29, 1868.*

Brevet Colonel George A. Forsyth, Commanding Detachment of Scouts :

I would suggest that you move across the head-waters of Solomon (river) to Beaver Creek, thence down that creek to Fort Wallace. On arrival at Wallace report to me by telegraph at this place.

Yours truly,

P. H. SHERIDAN, Major-General.

Shaking hands with the genial colonel, who wished me all sorts of good luck, I sprang into the saddle with a light heart, and no little elation, at the thought of having a field command and a roving commission—a state of affairs that any true cavalry man can thoroughly appreciate. In less than ten hours' time we were practically beyond civilization and well into the Indian country. Looking back, at this late day, after more than twenty-five years have passed since the morning we left Fort Hays for the head-waters of the Solomon River, I find it almost impossible not to rhapsodize somewhat over the freedom of the life we led: the fresh air of the plains, the clearness of the atmosphere, the herds of buffalo, which scarcely raised their heads from their feeding-grounds as we passed, the bands of antelope that circled around us, the chirping bark of the prairie-dogs as they plunged headlong into their holes as we approached, the shout that startled the sneaking gray wolf into a run, the laugh that followed the antics of our pack-mules, the half haze, half vapory mist that marked the line of the Smoky Hill River, and, above all, the feeling that civilization was behind us, and the fascination that the danger of campaigning in an enemy's country ever holds for a soldier was before us.

Crossing the Saline River and south fork of the Solomon, we struck Beaver Creek where Short Nose Creek empties into it. Here the Indians had evidently held a great sun-dance, where probably they had finally decided to go to war with the whites. Moving thence up Beaver Creek, beyond timber-line, I struck trail directly for Fort Wallace, reaching there the night of September 5th, not having seen an Indian during the march. Here I found a messenger from the governor of the State of Kansas, urging me to move to the protection of some settlers in Bison Basin. This I decided to do, with the co-operation of Colonel Bankhead, the commanding officer at Wallace, and so telegraphed the commanding general of the department; but as the command was about starting word was received from the little town of Sheridan, thirteen miles east from Wallace, and then at the end of the Kansas Pacific Railroad, that the Indians had attacked a freighter's train near there, killed two of the teamsters, and captured some of their teams. Leaving two of my command sick in hospital at Wallace, I started at once for the scene of action. On my arrival there I carefully examined the ground in the vicinity, and soon reached the conclusion that the attack had been made by a war party of not more than twenty or twenty-five Indians—this from the fact that there were not more than thirty or thirty-five different-sized pony tracks to be seen; and as the ground near where the wagon train had been fired upon was slightly marshy, the impress of the hoofs of the horses of their assailants was very distinct and easily compared, and the result was as I have stated. Little as I then knew, in comparison with what I have since learned, of Indian habits, I knew that it was customary for a war party to drive with them a few extra horses, and I therefore made up my mind that while this party was probably not less than twenty, it did not exceed twenty-five men. This being the case, I assumed that the attack had been made by a scouting party, and not improbably by a war party who had cut my trail and followed it towards Fort Wallace, and stumbling upon this freight train, had at an opportune moment attempted its capture, but finding that the drivers were armed, and plucky enough to defend themselves, concluded not to risk a heavy loss, and accordingly drew off, after killing and scalping two poor teamsters, who had incautiously fallen behind the train a few moments before the attack was made. We followed the trail until dark, and camped upon it. Resuming our march at early dawn, we again took the trail, but within two hours it began to become less and less distinct; every few hundred yards it was a little less clearly apparent, and I realized that the Indians were dropping out here and there, one by one, wherever the ground hardened and their individual trail could not be easily followed. Riding together fifty yards ahead, Beecher and Grover kept their eyes fixed on the fast-diminishing trail; and knowing that either man was my superior in this especial line of plainscraft, I quietly followed on at the head of the command, content to await developments. Within an hour they halted, and as the command overtook them Beecher sententiously remarked:

"Disappeared!"

Halting and dismounting the command, we held a consultation, in which Grover, Beecher, McCall, and I took part.

On one point we were all agreed, and that was that the Indians had seen us, knew they were being followed, and had scattered on the trail, and it was reasonable to suppose that they would rejoin their main body sooner or later. One thing was certain: they were not strong enough to fight us. The question now was, would they willingly give us a trail to their main body? Evidently not, as their object was to throw us off the scent. If this conclusion was correct, was it not probable that if we could pick up their trail and find the rendezvous of the main body, we could successfully give them battle? Beecher said little, and refused to express an opinion. Grover and McCall were inclined to think that before we could overtake the war party it was more than probable that they would be able to mass several of the tribes against us, as the general trend of their trail was north, towards the Republican River. Now, I had already determined in my own mind that it was in that section of country we would eventually find the Sioux and Northern Cheyenne, who had recently done so much damage to the settlers near Bison Basin, and I therefore cut short the discussion by saying that I had determined to find and attack the Indians, no matter what the odds might be against us. If we could not defeat them, we would show them that the government did not propose that they should escape unpunished for want of energy in their pursuit. That I thought, with fifty-one men, even if we could not defeat them, they could not annihilate us. Furthermore, it was expected that the command would fight the Indians, and I meant it should do so. Pushing on to Short Nose Creek, and seeking for trails in every direction, on the fifth day out from Wallace, on the north bank of the Republican River, we stumbled upon an abandoned "wickie-up," a shelter formed by pressing over young willows, or alders, growing about three feet apart, interlacing the tops of their branches, and covering the top with hides or long swamp-grass. It had evidently been occupied by two dismounted Indians the preceding night, was carefully concealed in the swamp-willows, and an attempt of one of our party to push through the willow copse on the river-bank to get a drink for his horse discovered it. We took up the trail here, and followed it a couple of miles, and were rewarded by finding a place where three mounted Indians had encamped within twenty-four hours;

and following their trail, we ran into that of a small war party, possibly some of the Indians who had given us the slip a few days since. From this on the trail was easily followed. It led up to the forks of the Republican River, where it crossed to the north side of the stream, and grew steadily larger as various small trails from the north and south entered it, until finally it was a broad beaten road along which had been driven horses, cattle, and travois carrying heavy loads of Indian tent-poles that had worn great ruts into the earth, showing that all the paraphernalia of one or more large Indian villages had passed that way. Coming to what we then believed to be Delaware Creek, but which we knew later to be the Arickaree fork of the Republican River, we found the trail leading up it along the south bank of the stream. Encamping at nightfall, we again took up the march the next morning, and pushed steadily ahead. So far we had not seen an Indian, but the trail grew steadily broader until it was a well-beaten road, and some of the men of the command ventured to approach me with a protest. They said that if we followed the Indians to their villages we would be met with overwhelming numbers, and stood no show whatever for our lives. I listened to them patiently, told them that they were assuming no risk that I was not taking myself, that they had enrolled to fight Indians, and that, in my opinion, there was less danger to advance and attack than there would be now to attempt to return. This ended the discussion, and apparently satisfied that they had entered a protest, they fell back into the little column. The fact that probably half, or more, of my men had served as soldiers was, at this particular juncture, of great moment. These men recognized the value of implicit obedience without discussion, a truth that emphasizes the difference between an army and a mob. Each hour we progressed established the probability that we were following close on the heels of a large body of Indians, who could not be far ahead of us on the well-beaten trail. Here and there they dropped tent-poles, pieces of half-dried buffalo meat, now and then little articles of clothing, an old moccasin, a worn-out basket, and various odds and ends that attested their rapid flight; furthermore, no game had been seen for two days, an indication that it had been hunted away, and I now moved slowly and cautiously, fearing an ambush or a sudden attack.

In the afternoon comparatively fresh horse manure was seen on the trail, but not an Indian had been seen by a man of the command. That they had seen us, I felt convinced, and such I think was the general opinion of all the men. To say that I was altogether as satisfied with the appearance of things as I assumed to be, would not be the truth. We were nearly out of supplies, save salt and coffee; the Indians were an unknown quantity, and, from indications, were likely to prove rather a larger unknown quantity than I had expected to meet; but I felt the necessity of fighting them, and decided to do so, even though I doubted my force to be strong enough to do more than partially cripple them for the time being.

It was about four o'clock on the afternoon of the 16th of September that, as we followed the sinuosities of the trail, at a little distance from the south bank of the stream, as it wound in and out among wild-plum thickets, alder bushes, and swamp-willows, a bend in the river, as we passed through a little gorge, opened out upon a small well-grassed valley of perhaps two miles in length and nearly the same in width. From our side of the water the land sloped slowly down to the stream from the rolling plain on the south, while upon the other side it receded from the water at almost a dead level for nearly three-quarters of a mile, and then terminated in a line of low hills or bluffs, varying from forty to fifty feet in height, which shut out the view of the plains from that direction.

As I have already said, we were nearly out of supplies, save a little salt and coffee, and my animals had to subsist upon such grazing as we could find. As the grass at this spot was good upon each side of the stream, I decided to go into camp, graze my horses, refit my command as well as I could, and take the trail again early in the morning, feeling convinced that before the close of another day we would meet Indians. Dismounting about the middle of the valley, we encamped on the bank of the stream opposite the centre of a small island, which had been formed in the sand in the middle of the bed of the stream owing to a gravelly rift at its head, at which point the water divided and gently rippled along each side until it again united about two hundred and fifty feet below. It made a pretty break in the landscape, lying out in the bed of the main stream, perhaps seventy yards away from the river-bank on either side. All, or nearly all, of these western and southwestern streams are peculiar in one thing. In the spring and early summer, when the snows melt in the hills and mountains, they are deep, wide, and even majestic rivers. Late in the summer they dwindle to almost the merest thread of water. This stream formed no exception to the rule, and the little island in the centre of its bed was fully seventy yards from the bank on either side. It was raised about a foot above the water at its head, while on either side of it was flowing a stream of, say, fifteen feet in width, and with an average depth of less than five inches, that came together at the foot of the island, which here sloped down to the level of the bed of the main stream. Long sage-grass grew on its head, and a thicket of alder and willows shot up four or five feet in height about the centre, while just at its foot stood a young cottonwood-tree of about twenty feet in height.*

In western Kansas and Colorado, while the September days are generally hot, the nights are at

---

*This tree afterwards came into use for my especial benefit in a peculiar way. Assistant Surgeon J. A. Fitzgerald, who came out with Colonel L. H. Carpenter's command, had it cut down and, stripping off the bark, lined a section of it with cotton and placed my shattered leg in it, and in that way I rode in an ambulance over a hundred miles to Fort Wallace. Here we met Surgeon Morris J. Asch of the army, and it was owing to the unremitting care and splendid surgical ability of these two officers that I am now alive. Doctor Fitzgera d has joined the silent majority, but Dr. Asch (who resigned from the army in 1870) is still a practising physician in the city of New York. I wish here to put upon record my unqualified admiration of the medical department of the United States Army. The ability, training, and devotion to duty of its officers are worthy of all praise. Its post hospitals are models, and its care of the sick and wounded of the army, whenever it is able to reach the front, is all that could be desired. A number of years ago, while in Europe, I took occasion to compare the medical appliances of foreign garrisons with our own, and ours were greatly superior in every respect. It is to the credit of our government that it never spares money for medical appliances, supplies, and hospitals, but freely gives with a lavish hand where the welfare of its sick and wounded soldiers is concerned.

times decidedly cool—in fact, cold would not be an exaggeration of the truth—and in my wakeful hours of this September night, as I paced the ground to and fro along the river-bank in front of the line of my sleeping men, I felt that the coming winter's campaign in the Indian country would result in much hardship outside of actual fighting. I had seen personally to the posting of our sentries, and had given especial instructions not only to hobble the horses, but directed that every scout should be especially careful to see that his horse's lariat was perfectly knotted; and further than that, before lying down to sleep, he was to inspect his picket-pin, and see that it was firmly driven into the ground. In case of an attack, each man was to seize his horse's lariat as soon as he grasped his rifle, and to stand by his horse to prevent a stampede, for I was somewhat apprehensive of an attack at daylight. Several times during the night I rose and visited the sentries, for I was restless, anxious, and wakeful. At early dawn, as I was standing by a sentry near one of the outposts, closely scanning the sky-line between ourselves and the rising ground to our right which lay furthest up the stream, I suddenly caught sight of an object moving stealthily between us and the horizon. At the same moment the sentry saw it, and simultaneously cocking our rifles, we stood alert, with straining eyes and listening ears. An instant later the soft thud of unshod horses' hoofs upon the turf came to our ears, and peering just above the crest of the rising ground between us and the horizon, we caught sight of waving feathers crowning the scalp-locks of three mounted warriors. The sharp crack of our rifles rang out almost simultaneously, and, with the cry of " Indians! Turn out! Indians!" we ran backward towards our camp, firing as we ran at a group of mounted warriors which instantly surmounted the hill, where, pausing for a few seconds, evidently for reinforcements, they broke into a gallop and came rushing down on our camp, shouting, and beating Indian drums, and rattling dried hides, in an endeavor to stampede our horses; but by this time nearly every man was standing with his horse's lariat wrapped around his left arm, and ready for a shot at the stampeding party as they bore down upon us. A scattering volley from the scouts dropped one of their number from his saddle, and they sheered off, carrying with them two of our four mules, and two horses that had not been securely picketed, in violation of orders. The attempted stampede had proved a failure. " Saddle up quickly, men!" was my next order, and in an incredibly short time the command was saddled and bridled, and in another moment every man was fully and completely equipped. The two men whose horses were stampeded, owing to their own negligence, started on a run towards where they had disappeared, evidently thinking that there was a possibility of their recovery. Ordering them back with a few sharp words, I told the men to stand to horse, having already made up my mind what course to pursue in case I was heavily outnumbered. It had begun to be light enough by this time to see dimly surrounding objects within a few hundred yards, when suddenly Grover, who stood by my side, placed his hand on my shoulder and said, " Oh, heavens, general, look at the Indians!"

Well might he say " look at the Indians!" The ground seemed to grow them. They appeared to start out of the very earth. On foot and on horseback, from over the hills, out of the thickets, from the bed of the stream, from the north, south, and west, along the opposite bank, and out of the long grass on every side of us, with wild cries of exultation, they pressed towards us. A few sharp volleys from the command, who stood coolly to horse, each man having his bridle thrown over his left arm, staggered them for a moment, and then they hastily fell back out of range. It was scarcely so much of a surprise party as they had planned, and they were somewhat astonished to find an active and respon-

THE SURPRISE

sive reception committee promptly on hand and ready to accord them a warm and enthusiastic welcome on their very first appearance.

I now saw clearly that there was but one course to take. So completely were we surrounded, and so greatly outnumbered, that our only hope lay in a successful defence, and I determined, in any event, that they should pay dearly for the lives of my scouts before ornamenting the ridge-poles of their lodges with our reeking scalps.

The command was ordered to lead their horses to the little island just in front of us, to form a circle facing outward, securely tie their horses to the bushes just outside of the circle so formed, throw themselves on the ground, and intrench themselves as rapidly as possible, two men working together, protecting each other in turn as they alternately threw up the earth to cover themselves. As we moved in almost a solid front to the little island, leading our horses, a few of our best shots, under Beecher, Grover, and McCall, kept up a rapid and steady fire from our flanks to cover the movement, which seemed for a few moments to puzzle the Indians, for they had apparently left the way open on the east, down the stream, and, I think, looked to see us mount and attempt a retreat that way; but I knew enough of Indian craft to be certain that the little gorge just around the bend of the stream in that direction would be lined with warriors, and I knew, furthermore, that once established on the island, there was no direction from which they could take us unawares during daylight. Three of our best men remained temporarily in the long grass on the bank of the river, covering the north end of the island, thereby holding in check any unusually adventurous warriors who might be inclined to attempt to crawl up that way through the river-bottom. Scarcely were the horses tied in a circle when the men threw themselves on the ground and began firing from beneath the animals, when it suddenly seemed to dawn upon the savages that they had been outgeneralled, for as we started towards the island, judging by their actions in signalling their comrades on the opposite bank, they fully expected that we would cross the stream. Now they saw their error, and also realized, too late, the mistake they had made in not occupying the island themselves. Apparently infuriated at their blunder, and almost instantly comprehending the advantage we would have should we fortify ourselves, they made a desperate onslaught upon us, their various chiefs riding rapidly around just outside of rifle range, and impetuously urging their dismounted warriors to close in upon us on all sides. Many of the mounted Indians sprang from their horses also, and running forward they lined both banks of the river, and from the reeds and long grass poured in a steady and galling fire upon us. A few of our men had been hit, one killed, and several more badly wounded; our horses were being shot down on all sides, the poor animals plunging and rearing at their tethers, and adding their cries to the wild shouts of the savages and the steady crack of the rifles on every side. At the height of this crisis—for to us it was the crisis of the day—one of them shouted:

"Don't let's stay here and be shot down like dogs! Will any man try for the opposite bank with me?"

"I will," answered some one from the opposite side of the circle.

"Stay where you are, men. It's our only chance," I shouted, as I stood in the centre of the command, revolver in hand. "I'll shoot down any man who attempts to leave the island."

"And so will I," shouted McCall.

"You addle-headed fools, have you no sense?" called out Beecher, whose every shot was as carefully and coolly aimed as though he was shooting at a target.

"Steady, men! steady, now! Aim low. Don't throw away a shot," was my oft-repeated command, in which I was seconded by Beecher, Mc-

Call, and Grover. "Get down to your work, men. Don't shoot unless you can see something to hit. Don't throw away your ammunition, for our lives may depend upon how we husband it."

This was my constantly iterated and reiterated command for the first twenty minutes of the attack. And now discipline began to tell. Many an Indian had fallen to the rear badly wounded, and some had been borne back dead, judging from the wild wails of the women and children, who could now be seen covering the bluffs back of the valley on the north side of the stream; and so hot had the scouts made it for the Indians close in on the river's bank that they had crawled back out of short range, evidently satisfied that it was safer, as far as they were concerned, to send their bullets from a longer distance. During this comparative lull in the fight the men were not idle, and with their butcher-knives to cut the sod, and their tin plates to throw up the sand, most of them had already scooped out a hole the length of their body, from eighteen inches to two feet in depth, and piling up the sand on the side facing the enemy, had an ample cover against rifle bullets. I still stood upright, walking from man to man, but from every side came appeals for me to lie down. As we were now in fairly good shape, and the men cool and determined, I did so. Scarcely had I lain down when I received a shot in the fore part of the right thigh, the bullet ranging upward; and notwithstanding it remained embedded in the flesh, it was by far the most painful wound I have ever received. For a moment I could not speak, so intense was the agony. Several of the men, knowing I was hit, called out to know if I still lived, but it was at least a full minute before I could command my voice and assure them I was not mortally hurt. In the meantime one or two Indians had crawled up on the lower end of the island, and, hidden by a few bushes, were annoying us very much. However, the elder Farley, who, with Harrington, Gantt, and Burke, had temporarily taken position close upon the bank of the river, saw the flash of one of their rifles from the centre of a little bush, and the next instant a bullet from his rifle went through the very middle of the bush and crashed into the brave's brain, and a wild half-smothered shriek told us that there was one less of our enemies to encounter. As we heard nothing more from the other one, I concluded that he dare not again risk exposing his position by using his rifle. As I was now about the only man of the command unprotected by a rifle-pit, Doctor Mooers (who had been doing splendid service with his rifle, as he was a capital shot) suggested the enlarging of his pit to accommodate us both. Several of the men promptly went to his assistance in enlarging and deepening it; but while they were doing so, in leaning over to caution one of the men, who I thought was firing a little too fast for really good shooting, I was obliged, in order to ease my wounded thigh, to draw up my left leg as I lay prone on the earth, and, unfortunately for me, one of the Indians sent a bullet through it, breaking and shattering the bone badly about midway between the knee and ankle. Three minutes later I was pulled down into the now enlarged pit, and was under cover. Meanwhile a steady fire was kept up by the Indians, who, as one of the men expressed it, were fairly frothing at the mouth at our unexpected resistance, for, with their experience at Fort Phil Kearney, in 1866, where they annihilated a detachment of eighty-one soldiers in forty minutes, who advanced fresh from the post to attack them, the determined defence of our much smaller and rather worn party in the very heart of their own country was to them decidedly exasperating. In my present condition, with my left leg broken, and a bullet in my right thigh, I was, for the nonce, save for the fact that I still retained command, something of a spectator. Gradually working myself to one end of the pit on my elbows, dragging my body along with no inconsiderable pain, I was able to partially sit up, and, by resting my elbows against and upon the fresh earth, crane my head forward so as to obtain a clear view of the field. The pit occupied by Surgeon Mooers and myself was at the lower end of the island; consequently it commanded a view of the whole field. A glance over my own command was most reassuring. Each man was fairly well sheltered in a rifle-pit of his own construction, generally two men in a pit, and the various pits were in an irregular circle, about six feet apart, and fortified by an embankment of sand fully eighteen inches in thickness both front and rear, for the enemy's bullets came from all points of the compass. Some of the wounded men, with bandages around their heads, were quite as active and alert as their more fortunate companions. Only one man of the command had failed me; and he! Perhaps it may be as well to tell the story of this individual here as well as elsewhere. He had joined the command at Fort Hays, and I was much impressed by his appearance. No one seemed to know him, as he was a recent arrival in the post, and comparatively a stranger there. Tall, well built, brown hair and black eyes, a flowing beard midway to his waist, well mounted on his own horse, a good rider, and with a pleasing address, he not only impressed me favorably, but others also,

A FRONTIER FIGHT

On our first scout from Fort Hays to Fort Wallace he spoke of several Indian engagements in the far north in which he had taken part, and so won upon me by his statements and general bearing that I thought him, for this especial service, quite invaluuble. Something of a joker, he was rather inclined to guy and poke fun at some of the odd characters of the command, and especially at a young Jew of about nineteen or twenty, who had been enrolled just at the last moment at Fort Hays to complete the complement of fifty men. He was a short, stout, rather awkward and boyish young fellow, with cherry cheeks, and verdant in some ways, and entirely new to campaigning, but I soon noticed his good care of his horse, his strict obedience to orders, and his evident anxiety to learn his duty and do it. Furthermore, my experience with men of his race during the civil war, with a single exception, had strongly impressed me in their favor as being brave men and good soldiers. Imagine my surprise and astonishment, therefore, when we had been attacked at dawn, to discover that my fine-looking scout was an absolute failure and a coward. He seemed paralyzed with fear, and had been among the first to finish and occupy his rifle-pit on the island, and after firing a single shot he had lain sheltered in his pit, face downward, claiming that one of

the Indians "kept a bead drawn on him;" and
notwithstanding he was reviled and berated
roundly for a coward by the other man in the same
pit, as well as by those in his immediate vicinity,
while not a few sharply italicized expressions
were from time to time hurled at him by Grover,
McCall, and myself, he maintained his position
and still lay face downward in the sand, while
as for the little Jew! well, the Indian that from
dawn to dark was incautious enough to expose
any part of his person within the range of his
rifle had no cause to complain of a want of marked
attention on the part of that brave and active
young Israelite. In fact he most worthily proved
himself a gallant soldier among brave men.
And now I cautiously took in a complete view of
the field. Nearly all of our horses lay dead around
us; a few of them, badly wounded, still plunged
and moaned and strained at their lariats as bullet after bullet entered their bodies, and had I been
certain that I could spare the ammunition, I would
have directed my own men to put the poor beasts
out of their misery. Meanwhile the dead bodies
of their companions stopped many a bullet in-
tended for us. It must have been nearly or quite
eight o'clock in the morning. The cover of
any kind that commanded our island, such as
reeds, long grass, trees, turf, plum thickets, and
in some places small piles of stones and sand

thrown up hastily by themselves, was all fully occupied by the Indian riflemen, and here I desire to say that in the matter of arms and ammunition they were our equals in every respect. The Springfield breech-loaders they had captured at Fort Phil Kearney formed part of their equipment, as well as Henry, Remington, and Spencer rifles, for upon our withdrawal from the field, notwithstanding the fact that they generally keep their discharged shells for reloading, my command found scattered around in the grass many hundreds of the empty shells of fixed ammunition of all these different make of guns. Riding around just out of range of our rifles were several hundred mounted warriors, charging here and there, shouting, gesticulating, waving their rifles over their heads, and apparently half frenzied at the thought of the blunder they had made in permitting us to obtain possession of the island. Riding up and down their line was a warrior, evidently chief in command, of almost gigantic stature. I was almost certain who it must be, so calling out to Grover, I asked the question, "Is not the large warrior Roman Nose?"

"None other," was the reply. "There is not such another Indian on the plains."

"Then these are the northern Cheyenne?"

"Yes, and the Ogallalah and Brulé-Sioux,

and the dog soldiers,* as well. There are more than a thousand warriors here."

" I doubt that," was my reply.

" General, there are nearly five hundred of the northern Cheyenne alone here in the fight with Roman Nose," said Grover. I would not allow myself to believe his statement, and, furthermore, I did not wish the command to be disheartened, so I shouted back: " Nonsense! Grover. There are not more than five hundred warriors here altogether, if so many. You must be taking in some of the women and children," for just back of the mounted warriors the bluffs were covered with women and children watching the progress of the fight. A muttered reply from Grover, which I did not catch, convinced me that he still held to his first expressed opinion, while the men around me estimated the number far greater than either of us. I now know that Grover's estimate was very nearly correct.

For the next hour or so matters in our imme-

---

* " Dog soldiers " was a name given to about a hundred warriors of the various Sioux and other tribes that were for some reasons renegades and outcasts, in fact, bad men, generally criminals, who had been compelled to withdraw from association with their own people. Banded together, they were practically Indian highwaymen, and it was this band that the head men of the various tribes claimed they could not control, and upon whom they laid the blame for attacks upon the outer settlements when they wished to avoid responsibility.

diate vicinity were comparatively quiescent. A steady fire against us was constantly kept up by the enemy, but only returned by the scouts when they saw an opportunity to effectively use their cartridges; and the Indians at length began to perceive this, for as it was they were playing a losing game. Our men were now better protected than they were, and were also better shots. The consequence was that many a badly wounded brave fell to the rear, while very few of our people were being hurt. At this juncture the last of our horses went down, and one of the Indians shouted in English, "There goes the last damned horse, anyhow!" This rather confirmed me in the idea I had somehow imbibed during the action that either one of old Bent's sons (the half-breed Indian trader), who had been educated in the East, was with the Sioux, or else there was some white renegade in their ranks, for twice since the opening of the engagement I had distinctly heard the notes of an artillery bugle. Leaning too far forward to get a better view of the mounted warriors, who seemed to be moving towards the cañon below us, from where we had on the preceding day debouched into the little valley we were now besieged in, I rather rashly exposed my head, and some one of the Indian riflemen promptly sent an excellent line shot towards it. The bullet struck me just on the top of my soft felt hat, which, having a high crown, was fortunately doubled down, so it glanced off, cutting through several thicknesses of felt, but nevertheless knocked me almost senseless to the bottom of my rifle-pit. It was some seconds ere I could completely recover myself and crawl back to my sitting position. At the time of this occurrence I thought little of it; of course, a large lump swelled up at once, but as the skin was hardly broken, and just then I had many other things to occupy my attention, I took little heed of the intense headache that for a short time half blinded me. A month later, however, the surgeon's probe disclosed the fact that my skull had been fractured, and he removed a loose piece of it. About this time several of the mounted Indians, for some cause that I was not able to determine, dashed up within rifle range, and from their horses took a sort of pot-shot at us. Doctor Mooers, who had been closely watching their approach as they careered around the island, gradually lessening their distance, watched his opportunity and shot one of them through the head. As the brave fell dead from his horse he remarked, " That rascally redskin will not trouble us again." Almost immediately afterwards I heard the peculiar thud that tells the breaking of bone by a bullet. Turning to the doctor, I saw him put his

45

hand to his head, saying, " I'm hit," his head at the same time falling forward on the sand. Crawling to him, I pulled his body down into the pit and turned him upon his back, but I saw at once that there was no hope. A bullet had entered his forehead just over the eye, and the wound was mortal. He never spoke another rational word, but lingered nearly three days before dying. During the rest of this first day's fight he lay on his back opposite me at the other end of the rifle-pit, and several times during the day he partially revived, and then, probably in order to see if I was in the pit, and he was not abandoned, he would push his body forward and kick out with his foot, a half-unconscious proceeding on his part that caused me much pain. He could neither see nor hear, and yet he was evidently able in a dim way to reason regarding the situation.

Once more placing my back against the side of the rifle-pit, and again raising myself upon my elbows, I peered over the little earthwork with rather more caution than before. On looking towards the opposite bank, and down the stream, I saw most of the mounted warriors had disappeared, and those who remained were slowly trotting towards the little gorge I have before mentioned, and again I distinctly heard the clear notes of an artillery bugle. Others of the mounted warriors now moved towards the gorge, and it flashed upon me that Roman Nose was forming his warriors for a charge just around the bend of the river, out of sight, and beyond rifle range. I accordingly called out to Lieutenant Beecher, who was near the head of the island, stating my opinion. "I believe you are right," was his reply, and both Grover and McCall coincided with us. "Then let the men get ready," was my order. Accordingly each Spencer repeating rifle was charged at once, with six shots in the magazine and one in the barrel. The guns of the dead and mortally wounded were also loaded and laid close at hand, the men's revolvers carefully looked to and loosened in their belts, and word was passed not to attempt to return the fire of the dismounted Indians in case a mounted charge was made; but the men were told to turn towards the quarter from whence the charge came, and to commence firing at the word of command only. In the meantime the fire of the Indians lying around us had slackened and almost ceased. This only confirmed us in our anticipation, and word was again passed cautioning the men to lie close until the fire of the dismounted Indians slackened.

We had not long to wait. A peal of the artillery bugle, and at a slow trot the mounted warriors came partially into view in an apparently solid mass at the foot of the valley, halting just by the mouth of the cañon on the opposite side of the river from which we had emerged the preceding day. I had placed my back firmly against my little earthwork; my rifle lay across my chest, and my revolver on the sand beside me. I could not do much, wounded as I was, but I recognized the fact that even a chance shot or two might possibly do good service in the work that the savages were about to cut out for us. Closely watching the mounted warriors, I saw their chief facing his command, and, by his gestures, evidently addressing them in a few impassioned words. Then waving his hand in our direction, he turned his horse's head towards us, and at the word of command they broke at once into full gallop, heading straight for the foot of the island. I was right in my surmise; we were to be annihilated by being shot down as they rode over us. As Roman Nose dashed gallantly forward, and swept into the open at the head of his superb command, he was the very beau ideal of an Indian chief. Mounted on a large, clean-limbed chestnut horse, he sat well fcrward on his bare-backed charger, his knees passing under a horse-hair lariat that twice loosely encircled the animal's body, his horse's bridle grasped in his left hand, which was also closely wound in its flowing mane, and at the same time clutched his rifle at the guard, the butt of which lay partially upon and across the animal's neck, while its barrel, crossing diagonally in front of his body, rested slightly against the hollow of his left arm, leaving his right free to direct the course of his men. He was a man over six feet and three inches in height, beautifully formed, and, save for a crimson silk sash knotted around his waist, and his moccasins on his feet, perfectly naked. His face was hideously painted in alternate lines of red and black, and his head crowned with a magnificent war-bonnet, from which, just above his temples and curving slightly forward, stood up two short black buffalo horns, while its ample length of eagles' feathers and herons' plumes trailed wildly on the wind behind him; and as he came swiftly on at the head of his charging warriors, in all his barbaric strength and grandeur, he proudly rode that day the most perfect type of a savage warrior it has been my lot to see. Turning his face for an instant towards the women and children of the united tribes, who literally by thousands were watching the fight from the crest of the low bluffs back from the river's bank, he raised his right arm and waved his hand with a royal gesture in answer to their wild cries of rage and encouragement as he and his command swept down upon us; and again facing squarely towards where we lay, he drew his body to its full height and shook his clinched fist defiantly at us; then throwing back his head and glancing skywards, he suddenly struck the palm of his hand across his mouth and gave tongue to a war-cry that I have never yet heard equalled in power and intensity. Scarcely had its echoes reached the river's bank when it was caught up by each and every one of the charging warriors with an energy that baffles description, and answered back with blood-curdling yells of exultation and prospective vengeance by the women and children on the river's bluffs and by the Indians who lay in ambush around us. On they came at a swinging gallop, rending the air with their wild war-whoops, each individual warrior in all his bravery of war-paint and long braided scalp-lock tipped with eagles' feathers, and all stark naked but for their cartridge-belts and moccasins, keeping their line almost perfectly, with a front of about sixty men, all riding bareback, with only loose lariats about their horses' bodies, about a yard apart, and with a depth of six or seven ranks, forming together a compact body of massive fighting strength, and of almost resistless weight. " Boldly they rode, and well," with their horses' bridles in their left hands, while with their right they grasped their rifles at the guard and held them squarely in front of themselves, resting lightly upon their horses' necks.

THE DEFIANCE OF ROMAN NOSE

A FRONTIER FIGHT

Riding about five paces in front of the centre of the line, and twirling his heavy Springfield rifle around his head as if it were a wisp of straw (probably one of those he had captured at the Fort Phil Kearney massacre), Roman Nose recklessly led the charge with a bravery that could only be equalled but not excelled, while their medicine-man, an equally brave but older chief, rode slightly in advance of the left of the charging column. To say that I was surprised at this splendid exhibition of pluck and discipline, is to put it mildly, and to put it, further, that for an instant or two I was fairly lost in admiration of the glorious charge, is simply to state the truth, for it was far and away beyond anything I had heard of, read about, or even imagined regarding Indian warfare. A quick backward glance at my men was most reassuring. Each scout had turned in his rifle-pit towards the direction from which the charge was coming. Crouching low, and leaning forward, with their knees well under them, their rifles grasped with a grip of steel in their brown sinewy hands, their chests heaving with excitement, their teeth set hard, their nostrils aquiver, their bronzed countenances fairly aflame, and their eyes flashing fire, they grimly lay waiting the word of command, as brave and gallant a little company of men as ever yet upheld the reputation of Anglo-

Saxon courage. No sooner were the charging warriors fairly under way than a withering fire was suddenly poured in upon us by those of the Indians who lay in ambush around us intently watching our every movement, in the vain hope that they might sufficiently cow us to protect their charging column against our rifles. I had expected this action, but I well knew that once their horsemen came within a certain radius their fire must cease. For eight or ten seconds it seemed to rain bullets, and then came a sudden lull. Sitting upright in my pit as well as I was able, and leaning backward on my elbows, I shouted, " Now!" and " Now!" was echoed by Beecher, McCall, and Grover. Instantly the scouts were on their knees, with their rifles at their shoulders. A quick flash of their eyes along the barrels, and forty good men and true sent their first of seven successive volleys into the ranks of the charging warriors.

Crash !

On they come, answering back the first volley with a ringing war-whoop.

Crash !

And now I begin to see falling warriors, ay, and horses too; but still they sweep forward with yet wilder yells.

Crash !

They seem to be fairly falling over each other;

both men and horses are down in heaps, and wild shrieks from the women and children on the hills proclaim that they too see the slaughter of their braves; but still they come.

Crash !

They have ceased to yell, but yet come bravely on. What? No! Yes, down goes their medicine-man; but Roman Nose still recklessly leads the column. But now I can see great gaps in their ranks, showing that our bullets have told heavily among them.

Crash !

Can I believe my eyes? Roman Nose is down! He and his horse lie dead together on the sand, and for an instant the column shakes; but a hundred yards more and they are upon us!

Crash !

They stagger! They half draw rein! They hesitate! They are breaking!

Crash !

And like an angry wave that hurls itself upon a mighty rock and breaks upon its rugged front, the Indians divide each side of the little breastwork, throw themselves almost beneath the off side of their chargers, and with hoarse cries of rage and anguish break for either bank of the river, and scatter wildly in every direction, as the scouts, springing to their feet with a ringing cheer, pour in volley after volley from their revolvers almost in the very faces of their now demoralized and retreating foe.

"Down, men! lie down!" I fairly shriek. "Get down! *down* for your lives!" cries McCall. And the men, hurling bitter taunts and imprecations after the retreating savages, throw themselves, panting, flat on their faces inside of their rifle-pits just in time to escape a scorching volley from the Indians still lying in ambush around us, who have been anxiously watching the charge and, naturally enough, are wildly enraged at its failure.

As for myself, a single shot from my rifle, and a few from my revolver just at the close of the charge, was all that I could do in my crippled state; but the fact that I had to lie flat upon my back, craning my head forward, had, by placing me below the plane of fire, enabled me to watch every phase of the Indians' desperate charge.

But now, to me, came the hardest blow of the whole day. Lieutenant Beecher rose from his rifle-pit, and, leaning on his rifle, half staggered, half dragged himself to where I lay, and calmly lying down by my side, with his face turned downward on his arm, said, quietly and simply: "I have my death-wound, General. I am shot in the side, and dying."

"Oh no, Beecher—no! It can't be as bad as that!"

"Yes. Good-night." And then he immediately sank into half-unconsciousness. In a few moments I heard him murmur, "My poor mother"; and then he soon grew slightly delirious, and at times I could hear him talking in a semi-unconscious manner about the fight; but he was never again fully conscious, and at sunset his life went out. And thus perished one of the best and bravest officers in the United States army.

Once more I slowly worked my way back against the end of the pit, and leaning my elbow back against its side, craned my head forward for a view of the field. Close to our pits—so close that the men by leaning forward could touch their bodies with their rifles—lay three dead warriors; just beyond these lay several more, while for six or seven hundred yards in the direction from which the charge had been made the ground was strewn here and there by dead Indians and horses, singly and in little groups, showing clearly the effect of each one of the seven volleys the scouts had poured into the charging column.

Turning towards where my guide Grover lay, I somewhat anxiously put the question, " Can they do better than that, Grover?"

" I have been on the plains, man and boy, General, for more than thirty years, and I never saw anything like that before. I think they have done their level best," was his reply.

A FRONTIER FIGHT

" All right, then," was my response; " we are good for them." And again glancing to where lay the dead bodies of Roman Nose and the medicine-man, I felt that the outcome of the battle would be decided by the staying powers of the combatants.* In the meantime the valley was

* The following graphic sketch of this noted warrior is taken from General Fry's book, *Army Sacrifices*. It is from notes taken at the time by General Rodenbough, one of the army officers present on the occasion of a council between General Palmer of the United States Army and the Cheyennes, held near Fort Ellsworth, Kansas, in 1866, at the time this tribe entered its protest against the construction of the Pacific Railroad through their hunting-grounds. I regard it as the finest description of an Indian warrior I have ever read : " Roman Nose moved in a solemn and majestic manner to the centre of the chamber. He was one of the finest specimens of the untamed savage. It would be difficult to exaggerate in describing his superb physique. A veritable man of war, the shock of battle and scenes of carnage and cruelty were as the breath of his nostrils ; about thirty years of age, standing six feet three inches high, he towered, giant-like, above his companions. A grand head, with strongly marked features, lighted by a pair of fierce black eyes ; a large mouth with thin lips, through which gleamed rows of strong white teeth ; a Roman nose, with delicate nostrils like those of a thoroughbred horse, first attracted attention, while a broad chest, with symmetrical limbs, on which the muscles under the bronze of his skin stood out like twisted wire, were some of the points of this splendid animal. Clad in buckskin leggings and moccasins, elaborately embroidered with beads and feathers, with a single eagle feather in his scalp-lock, and that rarest of robes, a *white* buffalo, beautifully tanned and as soft as cashmere, thrown over his naked shoulders, he stood forth, the war-chief of the Cheyennes."

IN THE PITS

resonant with the shrieks of the women and children, who, from their coign of vantage on the hills, had safely but eagerly watched the result of Roman Nose's desperate charge; and now, as their fathers, sons, brothers, and lovers lay dead on the sands before them, their wild wails of passionate grief and agony fitfully rose and fell on the air in a prolonged and mournful cadence of rage and despair. And as for a short time many of the Indians rode circling around, yelling and waving their arms over their heads, hither and yon, apparently half dazed at the death of the medicine-man and their great war-chief, as well as at the disastrous failure of their charge, the whole scene, combined with the steady crack of the rifles of the Indians in ambush, the reply of the scouts, the smoke of the powder, and the view of the dead warriors and horses lying on the sand before us, seemed for a moment or two almost uncanny and weird in the extreme.

And now came another lull in the battle. The mounted Indians drew off to the little cañon where they had before formed for the charge, and for the next few hours were evidently in close consultation; but the wailing of the women and children never ceased, and the Indians in ambush fitfully fired now and then at our breastworks, but with no results so far as any loss to us was concerned.

About two o'clock, under new leaders, they essayed another charge, this time in open order, and half surrounding us as they came on. It was an abject failure, for they broke and ran before they came within a hundred yards of the island, and before they had lost more than eight or ten men killed and wounded; and not a man of my command was hit. Renewed wails from the women, and a desultory fire from the Indians surrounding us, were the outcome of this fiasco; but between five and six o'clock they again formed up in the little cañon, and with a rush came on *en masse* with wild cries for vengeance, evidently wrought up to frenzy by the wails and taunts of their women and children; but scarcely had they come within range when the scouts (who during the lull in the battle had securely covered themselves by deepening their rifle-pits and strengthening their earthworks, so that they were well protected from the Indian riflemen) began picking them off as coolly and deliberately as possible. It was simply death to advance, and they broke and fled just as the boldest of them had reached the foot of the island; and as they turned back and sought safety in flight I felt satisfied that it was the last attempt that would be made by mounted warriors to carry our little breastworks. Night came slowly down, and as darkness overshadowed the land it began to rain;

and never was night or rain more welcome, for during the day the sun had been intensely hot, blisteringly so, and our fight had been from early dawn without water or food of any kind, and we were wellnigh spent with the work and excitement of the day. As the Indians never attack at night, we were comparatively safe until morning; so, as soon as we had obtained water from the stream and quenched our thirst, I called McCall and Grover to me, and asked for a list of the killed and wounded, and in a few moments I had the result of the day's fighting, as far as we were concerned. Considering the fact that my command, including myself, only numbered fifty-one men, the outlook was somewhat dismal. Lieutenant Beecher, Surgeon Mooers, and scouts Chalmers Smith and Wilson were dead or dying; scouts Louis Farley and Bernard Day were mortally wounded; scouts O'Donnell, Davis, Tucker, Gantt, Clarke, Armstrong, Morton, and Violett severely, and scouts Harrington, Davenport, Halley, McLaughlin, Hudson Farley, McCall, and two others slightly wounded. As for myself, with a bullet in my right thigh, my left leg broken below the knee, and an inconvenient scalp wound that gave me an intense headache, it was all I could do to pull myself together and set about getting out of the dangerous position into which I had led my command. I had an abundance of ammunition and still twenty-eight fairly sound men, and at a pinch all but six or seven of the wounded could also take a hand if required in a hot fight. I had little to fear that the Indians would again assault our works, and I knew that water within our intrenchments could be had for the digging; in fact, Scout Burke had already dug a small well at the bottom of his rifle-pit, and with a shout had just announced that the water was rapidly seeping through the sand. The dead horses and mules would furnish us food for some days, if we could keep the meat from putrefying, and I believed I could rely upon some of the men to steal through the Indian lines and make their way to Fort Wallace, which I judged to be about one hundred and ten miles distant. Accordingly, orders were given to strengthen and connect all the rifle-pits; unsaddle the dead horses, and use the saddles to help build up our parapet; to dig out and fortify a place for the wounded, and dress their wounds as well as could be done under our adverse circumstances; to deepen Burke's well; and to cut off a large quantity of steaks from the dead horses and mules, and to bury all the meat that we did not immediately need in the sand. The men worked with a will, and before midnight we were in very good shape. I had volunteers in plenty to go to Fort Wallace, and of these I selected two—Pierre

A FRONTIER FIGHT

Truedeau, an old and experienced trapper, and a young fellow named Jack Stillwell, a handsome boy of about nineteen, with all the pluck and enthusiasm of an American frontier lad, who afterwards became one of the best-known and most reliable scouts on our northwestern frontier. Two better men for the purpose it would have been difficult to find. I gave Stillwell, as he was by far the more intelligent and better educated man of the two, my only map, told him about where I thought we were, and gave him directions to get to Fort Wallace as quickly as possible, tell Colonel Bankhead, the commanding officer, and an old friend, our situation, and as he would probably send, or more likely come at once to our rescue, to return with him and guide him to us.*   A little after midnight he and Truedeau stole out quietly, walking backward in their stocking feet, and carrying their boots slung around their necks, that the impress of their feet in the sand might make a similar mark to that of a moccasin, and deceive the Indians,

* These two men, Truedeau and Stillwell, eventually reached the post of Fort Wallace three days after leaving us.   They had to lie concealed during the day-time, as they almost ran into several Indian scouting parties, and at one time they had to conceal themselves by hiding inside the dried up, year-old carcasses of two dead buffaloes. Truedeau died a few years afterwards, but Jack Stillwell grew up to be one of the ablest and best-known scouts on the plains.

should they discover the sign. After they had started I ate a few mouthfuls of raw horse-flesh, drank nearly a canteen of water, dressed my wounds as well as I could with water dressings, and, a strong guard having been mounted, I dozed away until nearly daylight. Then we prepared a reception for our foes, who I knew would be likely to renew the attack at dawn.

All night long we could hear the Indians stealthily removing the dead bodies of their slain, and their camp resounded with the beat of drums and the death-wail of the mourners. I had cautioned the men to lie close, and not to fire until the Indians were fairly upon us, as I thought they would make a rush on us at the first flush of dawn. In this, however, I was mistaken, for from their actions they evidently believed that we had escaped under cover of night, and accordingly a large party of mounted warriors rode up to within a few hundred yards of our works, and about twenty dismounted and came running forward to pick up our trail. At this juncture some one of the men, probably by accident, discharged his piece. Instantly the dismounted Indians threw themselves flat on the ground, and the horsemen galloped off. Of course we opened fire upon them, but to little effect. I think we killed one man, but no more. I was much disappointed, as I felt we had lost an opportunity of crippling them badly. At daylight they again took up the fight from their former position in ambush, but as we were now fully protected, they did us no particular harm. It was now apparent that they meant to starve us out, for they made no further attempts to attack us openly.

As this second day wore on our wounded suffered very much. As I have mentioned in the preceding pages, the nights in southern Colorado during the month of September are really cold, but the clear sunny days are, in the sheltered valleys, intensely hot, and already the bodies of the dead horses lying around us began to swell and decompose. Our surgeon was senseless and slowly dying, and, unfortunately, in our rush for the island, we omitted to take the medical supplies; in fact, it was all we could do, in our haste, to throw the boxes containing our four thousand extra rounds of fixed ammunition on the saddles of four of our horses and get them over with us. The surgeon, in the panniers that were abandoned, had some bandages, his instruments, a few simple medicines, and some brandy; but these had fallen into the enemy's hands, and assuredly he had ample need of them. All day long the Indian women and children kept up a dismal wailing and beating of drums, the death-chant over their slain braves. In the meantime our men quietly kept watch

and ward, and rarely returned the fire of the be-
siegers unless opportunity offered to make their
bullets count, and during this day but one of the
command was hit, and the wound was a mere
scratch, and as nightfall drew on I felt satisfied
that the score was quite a long way in our favor.
Two more of my company were sent out at eleven
o'clock at night to try to make their way to Fort
Wallace, but they found the Indians guarding
every outlet, and returned to the command about
three the next morning.

The third day, fortunately, was slightly cloudy,
and consequently the wounded had something
of an easier time of it; besides, we had begun
to get used to our injuries. Desultory firing
was kept up by both sides from early light, but
with no great damage to either side, as the Indians had dug out rifle-pits for themselves, and
were about as well protected as we were. At
mid-day Scout Grover called my attention to the
fact that the women and children, who had been
such interested spectators of the fight since its
commencement, had ceased their chanting, and
were beginning to withdraw. To me this em-
phasized an idea that had taken possession of
my mind since daylight, viz., that the Indians
had about decided to give up the fight, and this
was still further confirmed by an attempt upon
their part to open communications with a white

flag. This was, as I knew, merely an effort on their part to get near enough to our works to see the condition of my command, consequently I directed several men to warn them, by waving their hands and shouting, not to attempt to come near us. They understood what was said to them, without doubt, especially as Grover addressed them in their own dialect; but affecting not to comprehend, they slowly advanced. I then ordered half a dozen shots sent in close to them. This action on our part convinced them that their ruse was useless, so, falling back out of range, their riflemen promptly sent several volleys into our works, probably as an evidence of their appreciation of our astuteness.

During the day I took out my memorandum-book and pencilled the following despatch:

ON DELAWARE CREEK, REPUBLICAN RIVER,
September 19, 1868.
To Colonel Bankhead, or Commanding Officer, Fort Wallace :
I sent you two messengers on the night of the 17th instant, informing you of my critical condition. I tried to send two more last night, but they did not succeed in passing the Indian pickets, and returned. If the others have not arrived, then hasten at once to my assistance. I have eight badly wounded and ten slightly wounded men to take in, and every animal I had was killed, save seven, which the Indians stampeded. Lieutenant Beecher is dead, and Acting Assistant Surgeon Mooers probably cannot live the night out. He was hit in the head Thursday, and has spoken but one rational word since. I am wounded in

E   65

two places—in the right thigh, and my left leg broken below the knee. The Cheyennes alone numbered 450, or more. Mr. Grover says they never fought so before. They were splendidly armed with Spencer and Henry rifles. We killed at least thirty-five of them, and wounded many more, besides killing and wounding a quantity of their stock. They carried off most of their killed during the night, but three of their men fell into our hands. I am on a little island, and have still plenty of ammunition left. We are living on mule and horse-meat, and are entirely out of rations. If it was not for so many wounded, I would come in, and take the chances of whipping them if attacked. They are evidently sick of their bargain.

I had two of the members of my company killed on the 17th, namely, William Wilson and George W. Chalmers. You had better start with not less than seventy-five men, and bring all the wagons and ambulances you can spare. Bring a six-pound howitzer with you. I can hold out here for six days longer if absolutely necessary, but please lose no time.

Very respectfully, your obedient servant,
GEORGE A. FORSYTH,
U. S. Army, Commanding Co. Scouts.

P. S.—My surgeon having been mortally wounded, none of my wounded men have had their wounds dressed yet, so please bring out a surgeon with you.

At nightfall I confided it to two of my best men —Donovan and Pliley—with the same general instructions I had given Stillwell two days previously. Shortly after midnight they left our intrenchments, and as they did not return, I felt satisfied that they had eluded the Indians and were on their way to Fort Wallace. On the fourth day our sufferings were intense. It was very hot, our meat had become putrid, some of the

THE DEFENCE FROM THE ISLAND

wounded were delirious, and the stench from the dead horses lying close around us was almost intolerable. As the ball in my right thigh had begun to pain me excessively, I decided to extract it. I appealed to several of the men to cut it out, but as soon as they saw how close it lay to the artery, they declined doing so, alleging that the risk was too great. However, I determined that it should come out, as I feared sloughing, and then the artery would probably break in any event; so taking my razor from my saddle-pocket, and getting two of the men to press the adjacent flesh back and draw it taut, I managed to cut it out myself without disturbing the artery, greatly to my almost immediate relief. At dawn of this day the Indian riflemen had sent in quite a volley, and at odd times kept sending in shots from their ambuscade; but they grew gradually less, and in the afternoon almost ceased. In the meantime but few Indians could be seen in the vicinity, and I began to suspect that the entire body was withdrawing. Accordingly, I asked several of the men to lift me upon a blanket, as by this time numbers of the scouts were standing upright, and two of them had crawled over to the south bank of the stream, and reported that there were no more Indians on that side. Just as the men had lifted me up that I might judge of the gen-

eral condition of things from a more extended
view than I could obtain lying upon my back
in the rifle-pit, about twenty shots were suddenly
sent in among us, and the man who had the cor-
ner of the blanket which supported my broken
leg dropped it and took to cover. The result was
that the bone parted and partially protruded
through the flesh. To say that I was angry is
hardly doing the subject justice, and I fear the
recording angel had no easy task to blot out the
numerous expletives with which I anathematized
the startled scout. This volley, which did no
particular harm, was about the last sent in upon
us; there were a few more stray shots sent at
us now and then, and we could see Indian ve-
dettes posted on the crest of the adjacent hills;
but save a few warriors that lingered around
in ambush to watch our movements, we did not
again see any large force of the savages.

Up to this time I have said nothing of the individual heroism of my men. It was worthy of
all praise. Young Hudson Farley, who was shot
through the shoulder, fought straight through
the first day's fight, never speaking of his condition until the list of casualties was called for.
Howard Morton lost one of his eyes by a bullet
that lodged just behind it, but wrapped a hand-
kerchief around his head and fought on steadily.
The elder Farley, though mortally wounded,

lay on one side and fought through the entire first day's fight. Harrington, with an arrow-point lodged squarely in his frontal bone, never ceased to bear his full share in the fray, and when a bullet ploughed across his forehead and dislodged the arrow-head, the two falling together to the ground, he wrapped a rag around his head and, though covered with blood, fought to the very close of the three days' fighting. McCall never once alluded to the fact that he was wounded until after nightfall; and so of Davis, Clarke, Gantt, and others.

There were, as a matter of course, queer episodes during the siege. On the third day a large and very fleshy Indian, having, as he thought, placed himself just out of range, taunted and insulted us in every possible way. He was perfectly naked, and his gestures especially were exceedingly exasperating. Not being in a particularly happy frame of mind, the man's actions annoyed me excessively. Now we had in the command three Springfield breech-loading rifles which I knew would carry several hundred yards farther than our Spencer rifles. I accordingly directed that the men using these guns should sight them at their limit—1200 yards—and aim well over the sight, and see if by some chance we might not stop the antics of this outrageously insulting savage. At the crack of the three rifles he sprang into the air with a yell of seemingly both surprise and anguish, and rolled over stone dead, while the Indians in his vicinity scattered in every direction, and this almost unexpected result of our small volley was a matter of intense satisfaction to all of us.

And now came a time of weary waiting and comparative inaction that was hard to bear, and under our peculiar circumstances wellnigh intolerable. We were out of food of any kind; the meat cut from the dead mules and horses had become putrid, and although we boiled it and sprinkled gunpowder upon it, it was not palatable. One of the scouts succeeded in shooting a little coyote, and not long ago one of my men told me that the head of that little gray wolf was boiled three successive times to extract the last shred of nutriment it contained. On the fifth or sixth day two of the command quietly stole away down the stream in the hope that they might possibly get a shot at some game, but their quest was in vain. However, they did find a few wild plums. These they brought back, boiled, and gave to the wounded, and I know that the few spoonfuls I received was by far the most delicious food that ever passed my lips. As the days wore on the wounded became feverish, and some of them delirious, gangrene set in, and I was distressed to find the wound in my leg infested with maggots. The well men, however, did all they could for us, and we tried to keep up our spirits as best we might. On the evening of the sixth day I called the sound men around me, and in a few words stated the facts in the case as they knew them. I told them that possibly the scouts who had been sent out from the command had failed to get through, and that we might not get the succor we hoped for. Furthermore, I thought that by moving out at night and keeping together they could make Fort Wallace, and, even if attacked, they had plenty of ammunition with which to defend themselves, and I believed that no ordinary scouting party of Indians would dare to attack them after their recent experience with us; furthermore, I did not believe that any Indians, other than those whom we had fought, were in our vicinity, and I doubted if those who might still be watching us were in any great numbers. Those of us who were wounded must take our chances. If relief came in time, well and good; if not, we were soldiers, and knew how to meet our fate. For a few seconds there was a dead silence, and then rose a hoarse cry of " Never! never! We'll stand by you, General, to the end!" and McCall voiced the sentiment of the men by saying, " We've fought together, and, by heaven, if need be, we'll die together!" The next two days seem to me to have been almost interminable. The well men of the command moved up and down the stream within sight of our earthworks, seeking, but not finding, game; at night the crests of the hills were dotted with wolves, who, attracted by the carrion, yet not daring to come within range of our rifles, sat up on their haunches and howled the night through; and during the day the sun beat down upon our devoted heads with a strength that I had not deemed possible in that latitude during the month of September. On the morning of the ninth day since the attack by the Indians one of the men near me suddenly sprang to his feet and, shading his eyes with his hand, shouted, "There are some moving objects on the far hills!" Instantly every man who could stand was on his feet gazing intensely in the direction indicated. In a few moments a general murmur ran through the command. "By the God above us, it's an ambulance!" shouts one of the men; and then went up a wild cheer that made the little valley ring, and strong men grasped hands, and then flung their arms around each other, and laughed and cried, and fairly danced and shouted again in glad relief of their long-pent-up feelings. It was a troop of the Tenth Cavalry, under Lieutenant-Colonel L. H. Carpenter, the advance of Colonel Bankhead's command from Fort Wallace, which that officer had fairly hurled forward as

THE RESCUE

soon as news of our situation reached him
through Donovan and Pliley. An hour later he
was at my side with his infantry, and in less
than another hour Colonel Brisbin, of the Second
Cavalry, was there with the advance of General
Bradley's command, which had also hurried to
my aid.

When Colonel Carpenter rode up to me, as I
lay half covered with sand in my rifle-pit, I affected to be reading an old novel that one of the
men had found in a saddle-pocket. It was only
affectation, though for I had all I could do to
keep from breaking down, as I was sore and
feverish and tired and hungry, and I had been
under a heavy strain from the opening of the
fight until his arrival.

During the fight I counted thirty-two dead
Indians; these I reported officially. My men
claimed to have counted far more, but these were
all that I saw lying dead and I have made it a
rule never to report a dead Indian I have not
seen myself. The troops who came to my rescue
unearthed many a one, and several years later
I met one of the younger chiefs of the Brulé-
Sioux at a grand buffalo-hunt given by General
Sheridan to the Grand Duke Alexis of Russia.
It was a superb affair, and a large number of
Indians participated in it, and afterwards gave
a war-dance for the entertainment of the distin-

guished guest. One evening one of the government scouts asked me if I would see this young chief, a man of about twenty-seven or twenty-eight years, who wished to talk with me about the fight on the Republican. We had a long, and to me, at least, an interesting, conversation over the affair. He asked me how many men I had, and I told him, and gave him a true account of those killed and wounded and I saw that he was much pleased. He told the interpreter that I told the truth, as he had counted my men himself; that for four days they had been watching my every movement, gathering their warriors to meet us from far and near, and that I stopped and encamped about two miles below where they lay in ambush for me. He said that had I continued my march for another hour the day I encamped at four o'clock in the afternoon, every man of us would have been slaughtered. My occupation of the island was a surprise to them all, and it was the only thing that saved us. I then questioned him regarding their numbers and losses. He hesitated for some time, but finally told the interpreter something, and the interpreter told me that there were nearly a thousand Indian warriors in the fight. He said he thought the number about nine hundred and seventy. Regarding their losses, the chief held up his two hands seven times together, and then one hand singly, which, the interpreter told me, signified seventy-five. I asked the interpreter if that meant killed and wounded. "That," said the interpreter, "signifies the killed only. He says there were 'heaps' wounded." Just as he started to go he stopped and spoke to the interpreter again. "He wishes to know whether you did not get enough of it," said the interpreter.

"Tell him yes, all I wanted," was my reply. "How about himself?"

As my words were interpreted he gave a grim, half-humorous look, and then, unfolding his blanket and opening the breast of his buckskin shirt, pointed to where a bullet had evidently gone through his lungs, nodded, closed his shirt, wrapped his blanket around him, turned and stalked quietly from the tent.

AN APACHE RAID

AN APACHE RAID

IN the spring of 1882 I was in command of six troops of the Fourth United States Cavalry in the field, on the line of the Southern Pacific Railroad, between the stations of Separ and Lordsburg, in the Territory of New Mexico.

Word had come to us that the renegade Apaches in Mexico were known to be contemplating a movement that might, and probably would, eventuate in their trying to enter the Apache Reservation at San Carlos, Arizona, and compel the reservation Indians to break out and go back to Mexico with them. This the authorities wished to prevent; consequently we lay close to the border-line and kept watch and ward along the Mexican frontier as well as we were able, for it is a line of country easily crossed, and there is no difficulty in a lone Indian scout keeping an eye on an organized force, unseen by it, and at night hurrying back to warn his war-party to ware danger; and the Apaches are all good scouts, and, as past masters in the art of deception, something more. For some years prior to the date of which I write the White Mountain Apaches had been waging a desultory but bloody warfare upon the ranchmen of the territories of New Mexico and Arizona, and so many times had they apparently accepted peace, only to break out again into open hostilities at the first favorable opportunity, that the exasperated settlers almost unanimously demanded their extermination; and from their stand-point much could have been said to justify such an extreme measure. Cruel, crafty, wary, quick to scent danger, equally active to discover a weak or exposed place within his reach, tireless when pursued, patient in defeat, and merciless in success, always seeking the maximum of gain at the minimum of risk, the Apache was well-named by the late General George Crook "the tiger of the human species."

Reckless to temerity in pursuit of a flying foe, should his enemy turn at bay, his pursuer instantly sought cover, and took no unavoidable risk for glory's sake. Yet, when finally driven to bay himself, he gave no evidence of fear, and dying like a warrior, only ceased fighting at his last gasp.

An Apache, once having shed the blood of a white man, whether in battle, in a foray against the ranchers, the capture of a stage-coach or freighters' train, or by the cowardly murder of some lone prospecting miner, seemed to develop an unquenchable desire for rapine and murder, and thenceforward grew moody, restless, and uneasy within the limits of his reservation, and sooner or later disappeared from it and joined the renegades who, in the times I write of, roamed at will among the rugged fastnesses of the Sierra Madre Mountains from twenty to fifty miles within the borders of old Mexico. This range of mountains varies in width from forty to one hundred and sixty miles, and in places is almost entirely uninhabited. From the comparative safety of this vantage-ground the renegade Apaches patiently waited an opportune moment to move quietly up to our line, avoiding the few Mexican mountain towns and outlying ranches and well-known trails, rarely or never following or even crossing a beaten path, but creeping through the unsettled stretches of the mountains and traversing the intervening valleys at night, concealed themselves well up in some cañon in the mountains within striking distance of the border, and lay concealed, resting, and waiting the return and report of their individual scouts; then, crossing our border at night, they halted in some unfrequented spot until early dawn, when, stealing closely down to some lone ranch, they lay in ambush until the ranchmen rode out upon the range, suddenly shot them down, raided the house, outraging and killing its inmates, plundered it of fire-arms and whatever else took their fancy, and then rode rapidly on to repeat the same scenes of plunder, outrage, and pillage at other outlying ranches along the route that they had previously marked out, leaving a bloody trail of dead men, women, and children to mark their course. They rarely spent more than one night within our borders, and it has happened that even before word reached the border settlements or frontier army posts they were already across the line back in old Mexico, and safe in their mountain eyrie, the only evidence of their work being the scenes of blood and desolation they left behind them. Is it to be wondered at that the frontiersmen were bitter?

On the 21st of April a telegram advised me that the renegade Apaches had appeared on the San Carlos Reservation, killed several whites, including the chief of the Indian police—a splendid young fellow named Sterling, who was fascinated with Indian life, and who had for some time been in command of a body of friendly Apache scouts—carried off Chief Loco's entire band, including the women and children, and having been joined by a number of the Chiricahua Apaches, had started back for Mexico. It was impossible to determine with accuracy the route they would take; but as the whole country was at this time unusually dry, many of the springs and water - holes having dried up, I thought it probable that they would follow the trend of the watercourses that would bring them nearest to the Mexican border, so I concluded that they would make for the Gila River, somewhere beyond the Steins Pass range of mountains, and try to get back that way. Before I had left my post, Fort Cummings, New Mexico, I had sent the Indian scouts stationed there out on a scout through the Hatchet Mountains, under Lieutenant C. S. Hall, of the Thirteenth Infantry, and I at once sent the above information to him, ordering him to join me in the field immediately. At Lordsburg I had a telegram from him, and replied to it by ordering him to join me at Richmond, on the Gila River, scouting the Burro Mountains en route.

I had gone to Lordsburg as soon as I could after receiving notice that the Apaches had been at San Carlos, and from there moved at once to Steins Pass range. Our Indian scouts could not find any trace of a recent Indian trail, so I concluded that they had not come up that way from Mexico. Knowing that there was not any water to be had at Steins Pass, I had directed a tank-car of water to be sent to the station there from San Simon station. We camped there on the night of the 22d, and made a dry camp. At 3.20

AN APACHE RAID

A.M. on the 23d we fed and groomed, and at four o'clock the welcome tank-car reached us, and the horses of the entire command were watered from camp-kettles—slow work, especially as the tank had only two faucets that could be used. Before six o'clock we started for Richmond, moving down into the plain and cutting directly across it, heading for the Richmond road. Before starting I ordered Lieutenant D. N. McDonald, of the Fourth Cavalry, to take six of the mounted scouts who had come from Fort Craig, New Mexico, and two enlisted men, and try to cut any Indian trails he might find along the southeastern end of Steins Pass range. At his especial request, I dismounted one of the other scouts and gave him our most reliable Apache scout, Yuma Bill, who spoke English very well, and was an unusually fine Indian, and I also sent our six dismounted scouts along the base of the same range. but further out among the foot-hills.

We had gone about three miles on our way, when Lieutenant McDonald sent word that he had struck a trail, twelve hours old, of ten dismounted Indians going in our direction, that is, towards the Gila River. I at once determined in my own mind that this was a party of renegades going up to help their comrades back to Mexico. It was an error on my part, for which I was afterwards heartily sorry. An hour later and I had

THE RIDE TO THE RESCUE

another despatch stating that fifteen more Indians had come in on the trail, having with them one mule and two horses, and were still tending northward. I sent two enlisted men back with his messenger, and continued my march. It was an intensely hot day, and the sun beat fiercely down, while the plain was baked to a thin crust everywhere. McDonald had turned the southern end of the pass, and was moving northwesterly along the base of the range, and the command was probably sixteen miles away, when a half-suppressed shout ran up from the rear of the column, and turning my head, I saw one of the Indian scouts, still nearly a mile away, riding at full speed for our column, lashing his horse at every stride and digging his heels into his sides with desperate energy, his long black hair waving wildly behind him, as he came towards us. In a moment more he had by words and signs told his tale. Lieutenant McDonald had been ambushed, Yuma Bill and three of the other scouts killed, and McDonald and his remaining men were in a rocky place trying to stand off a large body of Chiricahua Apaches. Instantly the bugles rang out, " Left turn, trot," and a few seconds later, "Gallop," and the command was speeding to the rescue.

As I have said, it was stiflingly hot. The sand of the plain, wet months before by a winter rain, had caked, and was crusted for an inch or so, and the stride of the horses broke it to bits as we swept over it. Each one of the troop commanders had turned on his own ground, so that we were galloping *en échelon*, and the sand rose up in clouds as we passed. Once one of my lieutenants, Mason, put his hand on my arm, saying, " Our horses can never live at this pace." " They must live till we reach McDonald," was my reply ; but I had little fear. The Fourth Cavalry mount was a splendid one, and the horses ever so fit and hard as nails for the work. It was a sixteen-mile gallop through sand and mesquite-bushes and little arroyas, and now and then over a stretch of stones washed from the mountains, rough and hot and fearfully dusty, and I doubt if those who swept across the Gila River plain into the foot-hills of Steins Pass range ever forget it. As we neared the base of the range we heard several shots, and glancing up, we saw Lieutenant McDonald riding along on the crest of one of the outlying spurs of the pass, waving his carbine as he came towards us. A hearty cheer broke from the command, for McDonald was a popular officer. I am now going to let him tell the story of the ambuscade almost in his own words, as he has kindly written out his experience on that occasion, and I can add nothing that is of so much interest as the bare facts.

AN APACHE RAID

LIEUTENANT MCDONALD'S STORY

I was ordered to take my six Apache scouts, including Yuma Bill, who was given me at my especial request, together with a corporal from my own troop, strike directly into the mountains, and search for a fresh trail of the hostiles, while the main command pushed out of the foot-hills and across the plain toward Richmond, a little settlement on the Gila River. Risk of the few for the good of the many in the military service is good for the many, but occasionally tough on the few. However, we struck into the heart of the range almost due north, and soon discovered the old Indian trail. It ran through the heaviest part of the mountains, passing over terribly rough places and through narrow gorges, where the chances for an ambuscade were so great that I experienced considerable difficulty in compelling the scouts to go forward. I changed the usual Indian tactics of following trail in file to sending one Indian, Yuma Bill, ahead, and scattering the rest right and left about one hundred yards apart, while I rode within a few yards of Bill, watching them all, and indicating to the flankers, when the trail led into a particularly dangerous place, to sweep out around and try to look in behind the position as far as possible to discover if an ambuscade were laid. All such movements were made at the best gait possible, considering the rough and rugged country we were passing over, and wherever we could do so we advanced rapidly from cover to cover, so as to lessen the danger of being hit by the bullet of any lurking foe.

Our manner of advance had been determined after a thorough consultation, and I had impressed it on the minds of the Indian scouts that my way was better than their own, as it was now nearly impossible for the Apaches to conceal themselves so as entirely to cover our approach and pick off more than one or two of our party, while, on the contrary, if we kept pretty well bunched they might get all of us. After we had gone some twelve miles on the trail we found a transverse ridge lying across the pathway, which ridge rose to a considerable height, and was capped with a rock palisade extending as far as we could see to the right and left, and this effectually cut off all flanking movements; but the trail at our front and centre ran through a gradually deepening and narrowing gorge between solid rock, until at the upper end the sides were quite high. Just beyond the top there floated the faintest, thinnest mist of smoke in the atmosphere, which would not be noticed by a tenderfoot, and which I could barely distinguish even when my eagle-eyed scouts had called my attention to it.

AN APACHE RAID

Yuma Bill and those nearest us said that the Apaches were up there in an ambuscade that they had laid for us; that there was no doubt about it; that a band of them had camped and cooked there the night before, and, on our approach being discovered, they put out and covered their fires, but had left a few faint indications behind them. It was not possible for us to get a view in behind their supposed position by the use of our flanking scouts, so the only approach was the narrow defile in front through which the trail led, and to follow it probably meant death to some of us, as the hostiles were supposed to be lying to the right and left of it on top of the high rocks, and would let us pass in and enclose us on all sides before opening fire.

To my order to go on, and explanation that a soldier had to risk his life if necessary to carry out his orders, they most solemnly demurred; neither would any single one consent to go through and develop the position on my promise to make all available dispositions to cover his retreat should he discover the enemy's position without being killed. I had sent off my corporal with a despatch, and he had not yet returned, so I was alone with the six Indians; and as neither force nor persuasion would avail, I finally taunted them as cowards and squaws, telling them that if they dared not go, their commander would,

and that he, for one, was not afraid of the Chiricahua Apaches. It being evident that a man
would have no chance mounted, I dismounted
and gave my bridle-rein to one of the scouts, and
instructed them to watch and give me what protection they could; but if I was killed, or so badly
wounded as to be unable to get back to them, to
keep together and defend themselves, and work
back to the cavalry command. After most carefully examining my arms, with my carbine in
hand, cocked and ready to fire at a flash, with a
great show of boldness I struck out on the trail,
indulging in a little parting bravado that I could
whip the whole Apache tribe.

Advancing into the defile, I soon lost sight of
the scouts, and as I approached the summit,
only a few yards at most could be seen either to
the front or rear, as the trail ran through a deep
and narrow passage with many turns and angles.
Constantly expecting to hear the sharp crack of
a rifle, I tried to see in front, behind, and above,
lest a hideous Apache should quietly poke his
gun over the edge of the chasm and shoot me in
the back. So, with every nerve strained to the
utmost tension, I cautiously crept from angle to
angle, crowding in against one side to avoid a
downward shot, yet frequently glancing at the
top of the opposite side of the defile to see if the
muzzle of a gun or an ugly Apache face might

show in that direction. Finally, reaching a point only a few feet from the mouth of the passage, I took shelter behind a projecting angle and peeped through the mouth or doorway, realizing that the passage ended abruptly at the end of the perpendicular walls, and that just beyond was a pretty little circular opening with a nearly smooth floor, walled in in every direction, the rocks decreasing in height as they approached the further side, finally falling away and leaving an open passage out right opposite my position. I could also see scattered about this circular basin several small mounds of ashes, showing where the Indian camp-fires had been. At this moment I was startled by the cracking of a twig under foot to the rear. Whirling instantly with cocked carbine, I saw Yuma Bill, his hand upheld in warning, who had become ashamed and followed me on the trail.

He advanced cautiously, furtively glancing around in every direction, closed in behind me and took a look at the little basin, and said, below his breath, " Apache there ; want you to come out." Whispering, " Be ready to shoot, Bill; I see if Apache here," I quickly crossed the space to the mouth of the defile, and then thrusting my head forward, I took one sweeping glance around. A few heaps of ashes, some Indian belongings used in camping scattered among the surrounding rocks—that was all. Bill came across to where I was, and I then stepped out several paces into the open, watching for a sign of the enemy. None appeared. In a moment I said, " Bill, me no believe Apache here." He sprang up on a projecting ledge, and looking across the open, said : "Yes, no Apache here— him gone. I see him trail go over there." An examination gave us a plain view of the trail going out of this basin, and with the eye we could follow it nearly a mile ahead, showing a different color in that soil, so unused to the footsteps of men. Examining the ground in the vicinity, Bill told me that the Apaches had lain in ambush here, but seeing the smoke from their camp-fires still hung over the place, had abandoned it.

Resuming our march, we followed the trail with flankers out as at first; within three miles, however, it grew larger by the addition of other Indians, and my scouts grew frightened and difficult to handle. The two Mojave Indians, especially the old one, Moh-kay-nay-hah (Mountain-deer Killer), were stampeded, and had such an influence over the younger one, Quay-day-lay-thay-go (Blood), that they lingered behind, and were of no use. It occurred to me, though, that in case we were attacked they would probably go back to the cavalry and give the alarm. On reaching the top of the first high ridge on

the eastern side of the range we could distinguish
the trail for a considerable distance. It seemed
to lead down the mountain-side towards the foot-
hills, as if tending towards the great Gila Plain,
in a northeasterly direction, where we could see
the line of the Gila River as it flowed down from
the mountains in New Mexico into Arizona.
Turning to Bill, I said: " Bill, Apaches cross
plain to Gila River to kill people in settlements!"
" Me think so, too," was the reply.

Just after we entered the foot-hills, on the
line of the trail, we came upon two mining prospectors with their burros. To say that they
were abject cowards and frightened almost out
their senses would not convey any idea of their
condition. These two men ran around in a small
circle, with their hands, jaws, and apparently
the very skin on their bodies shaking and quiver-
ing, the guns in their hands oscillating to and
fro like the hands of a palsied person. Perspira-
tion in huge drops ran down their faces, hair, and
beard, and they were utterly incapable of making
the very slightest defence. Although I stood before them in my uniform and spoke to them, telling them who we were, it was several moments
before they seemed to realize they were not to be
massacred. Finally I gave them a savage tongue-
lashing that brought them to somewhat, but I
could get no information from them, and telling

them that there were hostiles about, ordered them to pack up and go to Lordsburg, and stay there until the Indian troubles were over. This species of dementia from fear is not particularly new. I had seen it once before in one of my own sergeants, who on other occasions had shown himself a brave man, and I was destined to see it again before nightfall.

Going back to my scouts, who were laughing, Yuma Bill said, "White man heap scared; no catchum news!" "No, Bill, no catchum news; let's go catchum trail." But, naturally, instead of going back to the spot where we had left the trail, and where the two Mojave scouts were sitting on their horses, we moved obliquely to the front to cut it—myself, Bill, and the three other Yumas in front; the corporal, who had rejoined me, following on behind, the two Mojaves keeping their old position in the rear. Not cutting the trail as soon as we expected, Bill said that the Indians must have turned back into the mountains, and pointing to a great rock, several hundred feet in length, that lay at the base of a mountain spur at our left front, said that we would pick up the trail somewhere between us and that rock. I was much inclined to approach the rock in our former way, with flankers out to try and see behind it, but fearing that the scouts might doubt my courage from such precautions

in that locality, and my experience with Indians
having taught me that no leader whose courage
was doubted in the least could have any influence
over them, and having spent years with them,
studying their habits, customs, and language, I
thoroughly comprehended the importance of not
seeming to fear anything whatever; so I abandoned the idea, and, against my best intuitions,
we rode along grouped together, Yuma Bill on
my right, the other three on my left, with the
corporal in our rear. The trail was so obscure
that we were only a few feet from the rock when
Bill pointed it out as it skirted its base and
abruptly rounded its end, and then, immediately
looking to the right behind the eastward end of
the rock, he called out, " Two Indians," pointing
towards them. We all saw them; and then, in
compliance with my instructions that in case any
one saw the hostiles he was instantly to drop
back out of sight, but not to fire—signalling the
rest of us, who would watch the hostiles from concealment and learn what we could of them, while
a courier was sent to notify the main body and
bring it up—we drew quickly back and jammed
in together behind the rock, with our knees and
legs touching, bodies leaning forward, and heads
peering to the right to see what would develop
over there, half a mile away, where the two Indians were quietly walking along. This was

the natural thing to do, as the rock was so high that, sitting erect in our saddles, only our heads and a small portion of our bodies would have shown above it.

All this happened in a few seconds, and as the horses' heads reached the rock it brought us five abreast. It then seemed to occur to Yuma Bill that he had not looked over the rock; or he may have heard some noise, for he jerked his face so suddenly and quickly to the front that he came near striking it against mine as I was leaning looking to the right. I believe that the portion of a second that I gained in suddenly jerking my face out of the way and his looking over the top of the rock as quickly as he did saved my life, for in a flash I saw poked over the rock a thick array of gun-barrels, with twelve or fifteen Indian heads and faces showing behind them. At the same instant Bill cried out, in an intense shriek, as if it was one word, the sentence, " Watch out, Lieutenant McDonald!" Throwing myself forward on my horse's neck, I grasped the reins close to the bit on each side to turn him away, and then came the volley, and with the smoke in my face and eyes I threw my horse's head to the left-about, over the bodies of the three dead Yumas, that had been riding on my left, and had now fallen under his feet. I knew, from an exclamation, that Bill had been struck, and somehow was conscious that

THE AMBUSCADE

he had not fallen from his saddle. I heard the corporal, who, being a little behind and lower down the slope, had not been exposed to the volley, wheel to the rear and call, " Come on, Lieutenant," and I galloped after him, the three troop-horses that the dead scouts had ridden whirling and running abreast of me, as they had been drilled to do in the troop, and we made for a moment a correct set of fours, in retreat; but realizing that it would not do to go so rapidly, I called to the corporal to watch out for his horse, and began pulling in on my own, fearing he would fall in the descent and cripple both me and himself. Old Don was a splendid animal, but hard-mouthed, and I pulled so hard that I actually sprung one branch of a fine steel bit before I could stop him. When I had gotten, say, fifty yards away I came to a quick halt and wheeled left-about, getting a bullet through my hat as I did it, and another singed my jaw and neck.

At this moment a tremendous volley belched forth from just behind the rock, and I realized that there was another and much larger body of Indians lying there. Still, I took aim and fired at the Indians who were on top of the big rock shooting at us, and instantly they jumped, rolled and tumbled off in all directions, seeking safety; for Indians hunt cover always if it can be had. Just as I turned to face the enemy I saw a sight that

I shall never forget.   Yuma Bill had stopped and turned almost simultaneously with myself—possibly a second sooner.   As his horse halted, facing the foe, he rose upright in his stirrups, standing straight as an arrow, every nerve and muscle at full tension, his big eyes blazing, and his long black hair floating behind him, even his horse standing with the glory of the battle on him (and it is glorious, if cruel), with arched neck and fiery eyes, in an expectant attitude, ready to leap, but nevertheless standing stock-still, I saw Bill's long rifle come up swift and steady, but I saw no more.   I was closing the breech-block of my carbine and raising it to my shoulder.   I heard the report of Bill's gun, and immediately came the heavy volley I have mentioned, followed by my own shot, and the disappearance of the Indians on the rocks in front of me.

It was time to wheel now, and as I closed in my second cartridge I turned to the right-about looking for Bill.   There stood his horse with his neck distended and blood pouring from several wounds, Bill still in the saddle, but drooping forward, his head turning downward by the side of his horse's neck.   I saw his head touch the tip of the horse's mane, which was towards me, and I suppose he fell on his head, but I did not see him leave the saddle, for my horse turned and again dashed to the rear, and during the next three or four hundred yards splinters of rocks and gravel struck us both, thrown up by the hot fire of the Apaches. Catching up with the corporal, we turned again at 700 yards distance, and paused to see their location and judge of their number. I pulled out my watch and looked at the hour. We estimated the hostiles at 150, and saw that we had only struck the first point of the ambuscade. We had no time to linger, so I signalled the two Mojave scouts to join us, which they did. Then we came once more upon the two mining prospectors, who had heard the firing, and were again running around as before, moaning and crying. We put them upon the horses of the dead scouts, which had followed us, after I had taken my carbine and knocked a little sense into them, telling them to go to Lordsburg, and then I picked out a good position on which to build rifle-pits, when suddenly the young Mojave scout called my attention to some Indians running towards us through some mesquite-bushes. We first thought them hostiles, and were about to fire, when, to our delight, we saw that they were some of our own Indian scouts.

The old medicine-man, our oldest Mojave scout, was almost paralyzed with fear, and as the six scouts reached us he made the sign dead and continued to talk to them for a few seconds, and then these scouts, who had come to our rescue on hearing the firing, went all to pieces with fear, and began running around in the wildest excitement. Seeing that it would not take many seconds for them to become demoralized beyond control, I set in cursing roundly and abusing them for cowards, telling them to fight and kill the Apaches and not behave like squaws. Suddenly the largest Indian stripped off his blouse, and, naked to his gee-string, ejaculated, in stentorian tones, " I fight and kill Apache Chiricahua!" Instantly the others seemed to come to themselves, began to strip for battle, and in another moment were building rifle-pits at the places pointed out to them, with all possible energy. This big Indian told me that the command was away from the mountains, well out in the plain. I then mounted Qua-day-lay-thay-go on Jumping-Jack, our troop race-horse, which I had with me, and told him to find the command and tell General Forsyth our situation and bring the troops to our aid. Then I rearranged my Indians in their rifle-pits and had them build me one.

Meanwhile the hostiles, having despoiled and mutilated the bodies of the dead scouts, brought them out to where Yuma Bill lay dead, and, building a hot fire of dead amole-bushes, proceeded to have a wild dance around the roasting bodies of their enemies, occasionally running towards us, yelling and taunting us, and daring us to come out and fight them. I made a little speech to my scouts on the folly of being scared, and told them, holding up a single cartridge, that in case the Apaches attacked us after their dance, I wanted them to make sure each cartridge told on one of their enemies. I wound up by saying that I believed I could whip off the Apaches myself, and ordering them not to fire unless I should get up and run towards them, I crawled out 300 yards towards the Apache high carnival, and lying under a low-spreading mesquite-bush, very quietly and cautiously laid up a low breastwork of flat rock that was lying near me. Presently two Indians rode out from the group, which was not a thousand yards from where I lay, to a point 800 yards from our rifle-pits, and began pointing at them, talking and gesticulating, evidently about us. Raising my sights to 500 yards, I took deliberate aim at the one sitting still, looked up at the sky to see that my vision was clear, and once more scanned my sights, and seeing that I still held my gun exactly on him, I pulled the trigger slowly and steadily. A puff of smoke, a sharp report, and an Indian leaping up out of the saddle with a bounding motion similar to that of my three scouts killed at the big rock was the result, while the other one wheeled his pony and ran back at full speed, followed by the pony of his companion. My scouts saw him fall out of the saddle, and set up a perfect din of ear-splitting war-whoops as I walked back to them.

In the meantime we could see a great commotion and excitement among the hostiles. As we could as yet see nothing of the troops, the scouts seemed to have made up their minds that Quah-day-lay-thay-go had either been ambushed or run away, and begged me to take the corporal and bring up the cavalry, promising faithfully that if attacked they would defend themselves from the rifle-pits, and not retreat and be shot down like a band of antelope. The location of the rifle-pits was a good one, and they could not be assailed under cover in any direction; so, taking the corporal with me, we started nearly due east; but noticing, about a mile away on the plain we were heading for, a triangular-shaped mass that stood higher than the rest of the vicinity, I scented danger, so I turned our course southward, so as to pass the end of it 500 yards away. Sure enough, there sat and stood a bunch of Apaches, evidently put on watch to prevent any couriers being sent out from the rifle-pits. At the moment we saw them they were very much excited about something; their ponies were tethered near them, and they were gesticulating and talking excitedly, and even the watch who had been looking in our direction must have gone back to them, and so missed seeing us. The instant they saw us, however, there was a hubbub, shots were exchanged, and mounting their ponies, on they came, some fifteen or eighteen of them. We put our horses at a good gait, going a little south of our former course to avoid losing distance by enabling them to cut across a short angle and thereby gain on us.

We soon found that we had the better mounts and that they could not overtake us, so we kept well ahead of them, stopped to breathe our animals until they were within range, took a shot at them, and pushed on again. In about three miles we came out on the plain and struck what in the language of the frontier in those parts is called a " sliyer "—that is, the hard, sun-baked bed of a depression in the soil, only a few inches below the level of the surrounding plain, that in wet weather forms a lake, and in dry times becomes a flat, smooth, crusted surface. We made for the centre, dismounted, and prepared to fight, intending to kill our horses for breastworks if necessary; but as there was not even a blade of grass to protect them and afford cover in case they followed us, I doubted if they would dare to attempt an attack in the open. They stopped and gathered in council. Suddenly we heard firing down at the lower end of the sliyer, and saw dismounted Indians coming out on it, and our pursuers began slowly turning back towards the mountains. One Indian came dashing up on the only horse I had left back at the rifle-pits. I thought it was a hostile who had captured the horse and wished to deceive me, and was about to fire, when he gave the sign of friendship, and I realized he was the big Mojave scout. I asked what the firing was, and who were the Indians on the lower end of the sliyer. He told me that, hearing the report of our guns, the scouts determined to leave the pits and come to our assistance, and had been followed by the Apaches, and were now firing back at them. Happening to cast my eyes to the north over some sand-hills just below the sliyer, we could see a cloud of dust coming rapidly nearer us, and realizing that there was no danger of the hostiles coming any further, I galloped across the sliyer and dashed up the hill, and just beyond and below I saw six splendid cavalry troops in beautiful order *en échelon*, sweeping towards us at a full gallop. Quah-day-lay-thay-go had bravely performed his mission, but at the expense of the life of our plucky race-horse Jumping-Jack.

And now that the reader has Lieutenant McDonald's well-told tale of an Apache ambuscade, I will take up my narrative again. In a few words

AN APACHE RAID

Lieutenant McDonald told me what had happened, and moving my cavalry well up among the foot-hills, but just outside of rifle-range of the enemy, the order was given to dismount and prepare to fight on foot. The position occupied by the hostiles was a capital one. I found them strongly intrenched on the left side of Horse Shoe Cañon, and also in the middle of it, where there was an outlying mass of rugged rocks about four hundred feet in height, a smaller ledge of rocks about thirty feet in height connecting the two places. I formed two flanking parties of two troops each, left one troop with the horses, and moved directly on their front with the other. Major Wirt Davis opened the attack, and in about an hour, by hard work and good climbing, we compelled them to abandon their position and fall back. They then took up a second strong position, which we again flanked them out of, and gradually drove them back into the cañon and up among the high peaks of the range, some of them firing at us from points eight, twelve, and even sixteen hundred feet above us. I never saw a much more rugged place, nor one better adapted to the means of defence. We had forced them far up the cañon, and I regarded the affair about over, as we could no longer reach them.

The air was suffocatingly hot in the cañon, and we were weary and very thirsty. On one side of

the cañon, near its head, was a small spring of
water trickling into a little pool in the rocks, and
no sooner was it discerned by our skirmishers
than it was surrounded by men with canteens,
while others drank from the brim of their campaign hats, and again others threw themselves
flat on their faces and lapped up the water, while
others scooped up the precious fluid in their
hands.   Like a flash out of a clear sky came the
crack of five or six rifles, and bullets seemed to
strike everywhere around us, but no one was hit.
The way that thirsty crowd broke for cover was
astonishing.   In ten seconds every man was covered by a rock, and thirty men were scanning the
high cliffs on the opposite side of the cañon with
the keenest possible interest.   A puff of smoke
far up the side and a second volley was sent at us,
but ere its sound came echoing back thirty bullets
from as many carbines clipped the very edge of
the protecting ledge that partially covered the
Indians, and it must have hurt them, for it was
the last volley fired by the hostiles.   In this action I first saw the good effects of our (then new)
system of rifle practice.   Our men were far better
shots than the Indians, and kept them down and
under cover almost constantly.   Our loss in this
affair was slight: to the best of my recollection,
one non-commissioned officer, two privates, and
four scouts killed, and one commissioned officer

and six or eight men wounded. My men were very tired, especially from climbing through the crags. The Apaches abandoned thirty ponies and mules; those we did not need for the use of our scouts we killed.

Indian ponies that cannot be driven along with the command that captures them are killed, to prevent their being rounded up by Indian scouts, who, sooner or later, are always sent back on the trail with that object in view.

It was five o'clock in the afternoon when the affair was over, and as I had come to the conclusion that these Indians had come up from Mexico to help the hostiles down, I determined to go to Richmond, on the Gila River, where I had ordered Lieutenant Hall and his Indian scouts to meet me, expecting to find the hostiles there. I was moved to do this from the fact that Lieutenant McDonald had followed these Indians north on the trail. Major Davis thought I was wrong, and that the Indians we had been fighting were part of the hostile Apaches; but as we had not at any time caught a glimpse of Loco's women and children, I thought otherwise. After-events proved Major Davis in the right, to the extent that the raiding party was in the fight, but it had been joined here by reinforcements. We stopped for two hours, taking a much-needed rest, and after the horses were groomed we started for Richmond, and reached the main road, fourteen miles distant, at half-past one in the morning, having had to move slowly, as we were carrying some of our wounded on stretchers. Here I fell in with a citizen, who was on his way to Lordsburg, and he told me that the Indians had left the Gila River, after killing many people, and were on their way to Mexico. Furthermore, it was still eighteen miles to the river. I made a dry camp right where we were, as men and horses were very tired.

In the morning I was joined by Captain Gordon of the Sixth Cavalry with his troop, and Lieutenant Gatewood of the same regiment with his Indian scouts. First sending a detail with my wounded to Lordsburg, I at once started back on my trail, rested at Horse Shoe Cañon, where the men got coffee and groomed their tired horses. There were only two small springs here, and the men had barely enough water for coffee and to fill their canteens, but in every instance they divided their canteens of water with their suffering horses. We then pushed on to Steins Pass station, reaching there at half-past nine o'clock at night. I had sent a courier to Lordsburg with a telegraphic despatch to Separ station for supplies and two tank-cars of water, which I found awaiting us on our arrival. Our horses had travelled seventy-eight miles, sixteen at a gallop, in most intensely hot weather, and had been forty hours without water, save about a pint each at Horse Shoe Cañon. We managed to procure several barrels in which to water them, and it was piteous to hear them neigh and see them plunge as they heard the water rush into the barrels from the faucets, and they were held back until their turn came to be watered.

Despite the efforts of two men to restrain each horse, it was not an infrequent thing for them to plunge their heads in the water-barrel quite up to their ears in their eagerness to slake their intolerable thirst. It was half-past one in the morning before the last animal had been watered, and then the command turned in for a much-needed rest. At daylight I sent out the scouts to find the trail, as I knew that the retreating Apaches would cross the San Simon Valley for the Chiricahua range on the Mexican frontier, and all the men in camp set to work to shoe up our horses, as many of them needed looking after in that particular. At noon word was sent me that the trail had been found, crossing the railway about six miles west of where we were, on the old Fort Bowie road. At 12.40 the command was in the saddle and on the road to the trail. My scouts informed me that the hostiles had worked along the crest of the Steins Peak range, towards San Simon station, and crossed over the mountains, searching out a new and terribly rough trail down the side of a rugged mountain, only possible to be used by Indians who fully realized that their lives depended upon crossing the range without delay.

After the trail reached the San Simon Valley, instead of crossing the railroad at once, it led east among the foot-hills for eight miles, then crossed the railway and made directly across the valley for the Chiricahua range. It was a well-defined trail, and was easily followed until 6.30 P.M., when it scattered in every direction, and my scouts not being able to pick it up between the base of the range and where we were, I concluded it would be found leading southwest along the base of the Chiricahua range; and having heard that hostile Indians had been seen near Galeyville, a mining hamlet, the day before, and knowing that the only water to be had was in a stream—Turkey Creek—near that place, I pushed directly for that spot. We reached Turkey Creek at ten o'clock at night, and went into camp, having marched forty miles since noon. Half an hour later Captain Chaffee, of the Sixth Cavalry, with his troop and Lieutenant West's company of Indian scouts, came up, also in pursuit of the same body of Indians—his command appertaining to the Military Department of Arizona, while mine was under the authority of the commanding officer of the District of New Mexico. Information having reached me that the hostiles had killed some whites in the Pineries, a spot twelve miles from Galeyville, the preceding day, I sent an officer to Galeyville, about two miles from my camp, to ascertain its truth and get me a couple of guides.

At daylight we were off, leaving Captain Chaffee's command in camp, and the guides put us on the trail, the Indians having pushed through the foot-hills of the Chiricahua range, and then out into the San Simon Valley again. We followed it across the valley in a southeasterly direction, stopping to water the command at Cave Creek. Thence we moved to White Water Cañon, where the stream was dry, and rested an hour, and again took up the trail, which led directly over a range of mountains which is really an extension of the Steins Peak range. It was 9.30 P.M. when we reached the crest of the range, and as both the men and horses were pretty well exhausted, I made a dry camp. The day had been a trying one, and the command had been without water since 10 A.M., we having marched forty miles over a very rough country. At daylight we resumed the trail, which led down the mountain and out into the valley for some miles, where it suddenly disappeared. A careful search showed that the Indians had here scattered in every direction, and probably arranged to work back to the foot-hills individually, to throw any pursuing party off their trail. We moved back at once, but failed to find the trail again, even after long and diligent search, and as the men had been over thirty hours without cooked food and without water for over twenty-four, I moved down into the valley, and found a marshy place called Cloverdale Ciénagas, with a small stream of good water flowing out of it, and went into camp. I sent my chief of scouts out to look for the main trail.

At five o'clock in the afternoon Lieutenant Hall with his Indian scouts, who had been chasing me up for several days, reached my camp and told me that he had struck the trail ten miles distant, leading towards Guadalupe Pass. I was already aware that Captain Tupper, of the Sixth Cavalry, with two troops of his regiment and some Indian scouts, was ahead of me on that trail, as I had met a courier of his the preceding day with an open despatch stating that, in his opinion, the Indians were heading for the Guadalupe Pass, and that he, Tupper, would soon be down to the line. On the next day, the 27th inst., we moved down the Animas Valley towards Guadalupe Pass.

When near Cloverdale two citizens met us who told us that Captain Tupper passed in pursuit of the Indians the preceding day; that the Indians had moved toward Guadalupe Pass, and then, instead of going through it, had turned back, and moving almost east around the foot-hills of the mountains, had crossed directly over the range about midway between the San Luis and Guadalupe passes. They willingly guided us to the trail, saving us a ten-mile march by cutting directly across the valley to a point that they knew the hostiles had passed, and we pushed on across the Mexican line and over the range on one of the worst trails that I have ever seen or heard of. We reached the base about dark, and near the mouth of the cañon we found Captain Tupper and his command. He had been hot on the trail of the hostiles the preceding day, and reached his present location without the Indians being aware of his approach. His scouts located their camp that night eight miles distant in the valley, near a small ciénaga, or swamp, and before daylight he cautiously moved out and attacked them, hoping to surprise them, and did succeed in capturing part of their herd and killing some of them; but they managed to fall back and get into a mass of great rocky crags near the swamp, and his force was inadequate successfully to dislodge them. He had fallen back with the captured stock and his wounded men. We were now in Mexico, miles across the line, and I knew it, and, worse than all, I had strict orders in my possession on no

H 113

account to enter Mexican territory, as at that particular time relations were somewhat strained diplomatically in that direction, a certain agreement, running six months, I think, permitting the troops of either country to follow the raiding Apaches on either side of the line, having expired. and Mexican sentiment was against a renewal of it.

After thinking the matter over, I decided to follow the Indians. They had murdered and plundered our citizens, believing we dare not follow them into Mexico, and that once they were there they were safe. Captain Tupper had taught them otherwise, and I had determined from the start to follow them as far as I could, no matter where they went, as our people were entitled to government protection, and an imaginary line ought not to bar the pursuit of raiding savages. Furthermore, we were in a wild country, and might possibly find this band, and, with the force I could now control, defeat and completely scatter it, and get back to our own side of the line without the knowledge of the Mexican government. Accordingly, at daylight the entire command, including Captain Tupper's forces, moved out and down the valley to the scene of his fight on the previous day. The Indians had left their position in the rocks and started southward. We took up the trail and followed doggedly on.

About ten miles from where Captain Tupper's fight took place we found a poor old wounded squaw on the trail. She was very much frightened, expecting to be killed. She told us that Captain Tupper's command had killed six braves the preceding day, and they had lost thirteen killed at Horse Shoe Cañon, besides many wounded in both actions. Giving her some water and bread, we left her on the trail. About ten or eleven o'clock my attention was called to the dust thrown up by the Indians in retreat down the valley many miles away, the air being so clear that objects could easily be seen a great distance, and as there was no wind, a column of dust was visible a long way. Later on in the day I missed it, and wondered whether the Apaches had again taken to the mountains. On this day's march we also found the dead body of a warrior, who had died of his wounds, the wicker stretcher that lay by his side showing that he was of sufficient importance in rank for his companions to try and get him off, notwithstanding they were so sorely pressed by their pursuers. At nightfall we reached a small stream, which we rightly concluded must be the head-water of the Janos River. I felt confident that we would overtake the hostiles the next day, and so did all my officers. At daylight the next morning I heard the sound of reveille by Mexican bugles, and my command

had not moved out over a mile when Lieutenant
Hall, who had the advance, reported a Mexican
camp a few miles beyond.

After marching about two miles I was met by
Colonel Lorenzo Garcia, of the Sixth Mexican Infantry, who with his adjutant came across a
small ravine to meet our forces. He most courteously desired to know if I was aware that my
command was upon Mexican soil. If so, what
authority, if any, I had for crossing the line, as
I must know that his government had issued
stringent orders against any armed forces being
allowed to enter Mexico from the United States.
Quite as courteously, but nevertheless decidedly,
I told him that my orders looked to the capture
or extermination of a band of hostile Indians, part
of whom had come from Mexico, and who had
murdered citizens of the United States in the
Territories of Arizona and New Mexico, burned
their homes and stolen their cattle, and whom I
had pursued red-handed from our side of the border to the present spot ; that parts of my command had fought these Indians twice and followed them over two mountain ranges, and we
were still in pursuit of them ; that the citizens
of Arizona and New Mexico were terribly exasperated over these outrages, and righteously so ;
that these same Indians had for the two preceding years raided the said Territories and com-

mitted many murders and other atrocities, and finally taken refuge in Mexico; that my sole object was their pursuit and punishment, and that he might rest assured that no citizens of the republic of Mexico would be molested, harmed or injured in person or property by my command, but I felt it incumbent upon me to pursue and, if possible, destroy this band of murderers; the inhabitants of the border expected it of the troops, and we were anxious to fulfil their reasonable expectations. Colonel Garcia replied in substance as follows: " While I am willing to acknowledge the justice of your pursuit of these Indians, nevertheless my government is strong enough to punish these people." I replied that I did not doubt the good faith of the Mexican government, but the only way to get at these Indians was to follow their trail and fight them wherever found, no matter in what place or in what State or Territory. Our conversation continued for some time, Colonel Garcia, while very courteous in his manner, still insisting upon my immediate return with my troops to our side of the line, stating that the instructions of his government compelled him to take the ground that he did. Quite as courteously I replied that under existing circumstances I purposed to follow these savages to their lair if necessary and fight them wherever found. He then said: " If your sole object is the punishment of this band of marauders, it is already accomplished. My command fought, routed, and scattered them yesterday."

I then said that, such being the fact, my march southward was over, and I and my command would return immediately to the United States, but, with his permission, I would like to go over the battle-field. He very willingly consented, and we rode over it together. He had been advised of the Indians having gone on a raid to San Carlos, and was scouting the frontier, hoping to catch them on their way back. The preceding day he had seen a cloud of dust made by some parties rapidly hurrying down the valley, and at once concluded that it was the Indians on their return. Posting his troops along the trail, he attacked them suddenly and with great vigor; but the Apaches fought desperately for their lives, seeking cover and defending themselves to the last extremity. His command numbered less than two hundred and fifty, but they were well handled and behaved splendidly. In this action they had two officers and nineteen men killed, and three officers and thirteen men wounded. Quite a number of the younger warriors escaped during the fight, in which a number of women and children were also killed; but this could not have been avoided, as they took cover with the warriors. There were seventy-eight dead

Indians on the field and thirty-three women and children captives, among them the daughter of Chief Locos, of San Carlos Agency. She said that her father and his people were compelled to leave the agency by the Chiricahua Apaches, who came up from Mexico under command of Chiefs Chatto and Natchez, and she corroborated the statement of the old squaw regarding their losses at Horse Shoe Cañon and in Captain Tupper's fight. As the end I had in view was accomplished, I at once gave instructions directing the three troops of the Sixth Cavalry to return to their posts in Arizona by the route the command had entered Mexican territory, while I was to move with my own six troops to New Mexico by the shortest practicable route. Finding that the Mexican troops were without surgeons and medical supplies, I tendered the services of our surgeons, which Colonel Garcia was evidently pleased to accept, and the wounded were at once attended to and made as comfortable as possible under the circumstances. I also presented his command, in the name of my government, with some extra rations that I could now spare, especially as his own troops were on half rations and he had nothing with which to feed his captives.

I desire here to put upon record my warm personal admiration for the splendid work done by the Mexican troops and the good discipline of the command. Colonel Garcia informed me that so imperative were the orders of his government that he would have been compelled to oppose my further progress by force, though, as he admitted, with no reasonable hope of success against my larger command. Fortunately his brilliant fight of the previous day rendered such an advance unnecessary. He gave me a written protest against my presence on Mexican soil, and I submitted a formal reply in writing, stating the reasons I have already given for my being there. The officers and troops of both republics parted with cordial good-will, for this nearly annihilated band of Apaches had given the troops on both sides of the border many a hard day's work. My command encamped twenty-four miles north of the Janos River that night, and the next day we passed around the town of Janos, where all the church-bells were ringing in honor of Colonel Garcia's victory, leaving it two miles on our right, my reason for this being that I did not wish any of the troops to come into contact with Mexican citizens, fearing, possibly, some trouble. While passing Janos the commanding officer, Colonel Nieto, sent me by courier a written protest against the presence of our troops on Mexican soil, which I duly acknowledged, and proceeded on my way. That night the command encamped three miles below the town of Ascension, on the Coralitos River, having marched thirty-five miles; the next night we were at Mosquito Springs, forty-two miles from our previous camp, and the following day we recrossed the line into our own territory. So far as I know, only one man of my command had anything to do with the Mexicans, and he deserted while we were encamped near Ascension. This article is, as a matter of fact, the first public report of my movements across the Mexican line, my district commander, the late General Mackenzie, returning my official report to me, saying in substance that, owing to the peculiar state of feeling existing just at that time in Mexico, it was not unlikely I might find myself in trouble for my action. However, if the Mexicans did not make a direct complaint to the State Department, he should not take action, as the result justified the end; but the less said about it the better.

SHERIDAN'S RIDE

SHERIDAN'S RIDE

" When I heard this I took two of my aides-de-camp, Major George A. Forsyth and Captain Joseph O'Keeffe, and with twenty men from the escort started for the front." —*From the Personal Memoirs of P. H. Sheridan,* vol. ii., chapter iii., page 80.

IN the summer of 1864 I was on detached duty as an acting aide on the staff of Major-General Philip H. Sheridan, then in command of the Army of the Shenandoah. I was one of two officers who rode to the front with him " from Winchester down " on the 19th of October, 1864, the day of the battle of Cedar Creek, and purpose to tell the story of the ride from its inception to the close of the day on which it ended. I shall give, in sequence, the orders which practically compelled his absence from his army, show that he lost no time in returning to it, and state in detail his orders to me on the field of battle, and, to the best of my ability, show the condition of affairs as they existed on his reaching the army. If I am compelled to give myself undue prominence, please recollect that on the field I was only one of many aides sent here and there by the commanding general, and I can only tell of what passed between us, and what happened immediately under my own eye.

It seemed as though the campaign in the valley of the Shenandoah in the year 1864 was practically over. Twice within four days General Sheridan had attacked and defeated the Confederate army under General Early: first, on the 19th of September, at the crossing of Opequon Creek, in front of Winchester, Virginia, and again at Fisher's Hill, twenty-two miles further up the valley, on the 22d day of the same month. Both victories had been wrung from the enemy by dint of hard fighting and good judgment on the part of the commanding general of the United States forces, and his reputation as the commander of an army was now seemingly as secure as the brilliant record he had already made as a brigade, division, and corps commander.

The Federal troops lay quietly in camp in fancied security near Strasburg, just in rear of Cedar Creek, one of the tributaries of the Shenandoah River, and the shattered forces of the enemy were supposed to be somewhere in the vicinity of Gordonsville, Virginia; but the Confederate general, Jubal A. Early, was a soldier unused to defeat, a bitter enemy and a desperate foe, and, as later events went to show, an officer willing to risk his all on the mere possibility of regaining, by a sudden and unexpected blow, the lost prestige of himself and army. In my opinion, but for the opportune arrival of General Sheridan on the field of battle, there is no reasonable doubt that he would have succeeded in accomplishing his object.

So well satisfied was General Grant with the result of General Sheridan's campaign in the Shenandoah Valley that he thought he could with safety largely detach from the Army of the Shenandoah, and accordingly had directed that the Sixth Army Corps be returned to its old place with the Army of the Potomac, and he also contemplated withdrawing one division of the Nineteenth Army Corps to another field of duty. It may be as well to state here that there were only two divisions of the Nineteenth Corps with the Army of the Shenandoah, the other division being on duty in Louisiana.

Accordingly, on the 12th of October, orders were issued directing the Sixth Corps to march to Alexandria, Virginia, by the way of Ashby's Gap, and on the 13th instant it started, but events developed that induced General Sheridan to believe that it was possible that General Early had been reinforced, and he ordered it back the next day, especially as in addition to said developments he received the following telegram from General Halleck, the Chief of Staff of the Army:

WASHINGTON, D. C., *October* 12, 1864—12 M.
Major-General Sheridan, Strasburg :
General Grant wishes a position taken far enough south to serve as a base for future operations upon Gordonsville and Charlottesville. It must be strongly fortified and provisioned. Some point in the vicinity of Manassas Gap would seem best suited for all purposes. Colonel Alexander, of the Engineers, will be sent to consult with you as soon as you connect with General Augur.

H. W. HALLECK,
Major-General and Chief of Staff.

He informed the Chief of Staff of his action regarding this corps in the following despatch:

CEDAR CREEK, VA.,
October 13, 1864—9.30 A.M.
Maj. Gen. H. W. Halleck, Chief of Staff :
Your telegram dated 12 M. October 12th received. If any advance is to be made on Gordonsville and Charlottesville, it is not best to send troops away from my command, and I have therefore countermanded the order directing the Sixth Corps to march to Alexandria. I will go over and see General Augur and Colonel Alexander, and communicate with you from Rectortown.

P. H. SHERIDAN, Major-General.

And also despatched General Augur as follows:

CEDAR CREEK, *October* 13, 1864.
GENERAL,—News received from Washington since I wrote you last night makes it necessary for you to hold on to your present position at Rectortown. I will try and get over and see you either this evening or to-morrow.

P. H. SHERIDAN.

SHERIDAN'S RIDE

On the 14th he received the two following telegrams :

WAR DEPARTMENT, WASHINGTON, D. C.,
October 13, 1864.

Major-General Sheridan
(Care of General Augur) :

If you can come here a consultation on several points is extremely desirable. I propose to visit General Grant, and would like to see you first.

EDWIN M. STANTON, Secretary of War.

WASHINGTON, D. C., *October* 13, 1864—5 P.M.
(Via Rectortown and Harper's Ferry.)

Major-General Sheridan, Cedar Creek :

The Secretary of War wishes you to come to Washington for consultation if you can safely leave your command. General Grant's wishes about holding a position up the valley as a basis against Gordonsville, etc., and the difficulty of wagoning supplies in the winter, may change your views about the Manassas Gap road.

H. W. HALLECK,
Major-General and Chief of Staff.

The same day he wrote General Augur as follows :

CEDAR CREEK, *October* 14, 1864—3.30 P.M.

Major-General Augur, Rectortown :

GENERAL,—I got ready to go over and see you yesterday, and was on the point of starting when a force of rebel cavalry made its appearance in my front. I had sent a brigade, 700 strong, to go across the Shenandoah to establish a signal-station on the mountains to the left of Strasburg. The rebel cavalry opened three pieces of artillery on the party. I started a cavalry division across the creek on the Back road, and Crook sent a small division over towards Fisher's Hill for the purpose of developing the enemy's force. Up to that time he had shown nothing but cavalry. As Crook's

I   129

force pushed out, after crossing the creek toward Strasburg, the enemy moved out a strong infantry line of battle. After skirmishing for some time, Crook's command fell back to the north side of the creek. The indications last night were that the enemy were in force—infantry and cavalry, with artillery. The Sixth Army Corps, which started yesterday morning to march to Alexandria, was stopped and ordered back to Front Royal. It did not succeed in reaching Front Royal last night, but camped at Millwood. This corps was ordered up here this A.M., and reached this point about 12 M. to-day. During the night the enemy fell back. I had made arrangements to attack. I have not as yet made up my mind as to the intention of the enemy in making this move. I rather think that Early expected to find only Crook's command here. He was under the impression that I had gone over to the Orange and Alexandria Railroad, to operate on that line. Colonel Powell's division of cavalry is at Front Royal. You had better continue your work on the railroad. If required, I will send over more troops. I am very anxious to see you, and will try to get over to see you as soon as I possibly can.   P. H. SHERIDAN, Major-General.

The earnest desire for his presence in Washington is evident from the following telegram:

WAR DEPARTMENT, WASHINGTON,
October 14, 1864.
Major-General Augur, Rectortown :
Has General Sheridan reached you yet?
EDWIN M. STANTON,
Secretary of War.

On the 15th of October I was directed by Colonel J. W. Forsyth, General Sheridan's chief of staff, to accompany the commanding general, but I had no idea where he was going, and I had learned that it was useless to ask questions. I found, however, that only four of the staff were to go with him, viz., Colonel J. W. Forsyth, Captains M.·V. Sheridan and Joseph O'Keeffe, and myself. We took the road to Front Royal, accompanied by a large body of cavalry, and stopped at a farm-house that night. The next morning we again took up the march to Front Royal. While stopping near this place the general received from General Wright the following despatch:

HEADQUARTERS MIDDLE MILITARY DIVISION,
October 16, 1864.

Major-General P. H. Sheridan,
   Commanding Middle Military Division ⸆

GENERAL,—I enclose you despatch, which explains itself. If the enemy should be strongly reinforced in cavalry, he might, by turning our right, give us a great deal of trouble. I shall hold on here until the enemy's movements are developed, and shall only fear an attack on my right, which I shall make every preparation for guarding against and resisting.
   Very respectfully, your obedient servant,
                  H. G. WRIGHT,
                  Major-General, Commanding.

[Enclosure.]

Lieutenant-General Early ⸆

Be ready to move as soon as my forces join you, and we will crush Sheridan.
            LONGSTREET, Lieutenant-General.

This message was taken off the rebel signal-flag on Three-Top Mountain.

He replied to it as follows:

SHERIDAN'S RIDE

HEADQUARTERS MIDDLE MILITARY DIVISION,
FRONT ROYAL, *October* 16, 1864.
Major-General H. G. Wright,
  Commanding Sixth Army Corps :
  GENERAL,—The cavalry is all ordered back to you ;
make your position strong. If Longstreet's despatch is
true, he is under the impression that we have largely detached. I will go over to Augur, and may get additional
news. Close in Colonel Powell, who will be at this point. If
the enemy should make an advance, I know you will defeat
him. Look well to your ground and be well prepared. Get
up everything that can be spared. I will bring up all I can,
and will be up on Tuesday, if not sooner.
                      P. H. SHERIDAN, Major-General.

From this place we proceeded to Rectortown,
arriving there about noon. The following telegraphic despatches are self-explanatory:

WASHINGTON, D. C., *October* 16, 1864.
Major-General Augur, Rectortown :
  It is impossible to say how far the road is to be repaired
till we can have an interview with General Sheridan.
                      H. W. HALLECK,
                      Major-General and Chief of Staff.

RECTORTOWN, VA., *October* 16, 1864.
Major-General Halleck, Chief of Staff :
  General Sheridan just arrived here.
                      C. C. AUGUR, Major-General.

RECTORTOWN, VA., *October* 16, 1864—1.50 P.M.
Major-General Halleck, Chief of Staff :
  I have no cipher clerk here. An intercepted signal de-
spatch would indicate that Longstreet was marching to join
Early with considerable force, and was not far off. Have
you heard that any rebel force has been detached from

SHERIDAN'S RIDE

Richmond? Cipher despatches sent me yesterday or day before, via this place, were lost.

P. H. SHERIDAN, Major-General.

WASHINGTON, D. C., *October* 16, 1864—4 P.M.
Major-General Sheridan, Rectortown :

General Grant says that Longstreet brought with him no troops from Richmond, but I have very little confidence in the information collected at his headquarters. If you can leave your command with safety, come to Washington, as I wish to give you the views of the authorities here.

H. W. HALLECK,
Major-General and Chief of Staff.

From the above despatches it will be seen that General Sheridan could not well ignore the request of the Chief of Staff of the Army and of the Secretary of War to go to Washington. In fact, the statement of the Secretary of War, that he was only awaiting his (Sheridan's) arrival in order to confer with him prior to taking his own departure to confer with General Grant, practically settled the question. We pushed on from Rectortown, through Manassas Gap, to the terminus of the railroad then being in process of reconstruction, where we took the cars, with our respective mounts, for Washington, reaching the city at a fairly early hour in the morning of the 17th instant. After a hasty breakfast at Willard's Hotel, General Sheridan went at once to the War Department, and had a lengthy interview with the Chief of Staff of the Army and the officials of

133

the War Department, returning to the hotel shortly after twelve o'clock. We had lunch on his
arrival, and then went immediately to the Baltimore and Ohio depot, where a special train was
awaiting us, and at once started for Martinsburg.
This train was provided by order of the War Department at General Sheridan's especial request,
in order that no unnecessary time should be lost
in his return to the army. The Chief of Staff
of the Army sent the following despatch regarding the interview to General Grant:

WASHINGTON, *October* 17, 1864—12.30 P.M.
Lieutenant-General Grant, City Point:

General Sheridan has just been here. He has not yet
fully decided about the Manassas road, but will do so in a
day or two. He has gone back, with Colonels Alexander
and Thom, to make a fuller reconnoissance. . . .
H. W. HALLECK,
Major-General and Chief of Staff.

We arrived at Martinsburg after dark, where
we found an escort which had been ordered there
to meet us.* Early the next morning we started
by the valley turnpike for Winchester, twenty-
eight miles distant, reaching there about three in
the afternoon. We had with us on the ride Colonels Alexander and Thom, of the Engineer Corps,
who had accompanied the general from Washing-

* Captain M. V. Sheridan was left at this place to bring to
the front some members of Congress who were coming up to
visit the Army of the Shenandoah.

ton under special instructions from the War Department.

After lunch at the headquarters of Colonel Oliver Edwards, who was in command at Winchester, I accompanied General Sheridan and Colonels Alexander and Thom on an extended and careful survey of the country in the immediate vicinity of the town. We rode over the ground thoroughly, and it was dark ere we returned. I heard the matter of Winchester, as an available point of defence in case the Army of the Shenandoah was heavily depleted of its infantry, discussed freely; but I do not think the consensus of opinion was in its favor. Immediately on his arrival at Colonel Edwards's headquarters, General Sheridan had sent a despatch by courier to General Wright, at Cedar Creek, notifying him of his return thus far, and requesting any information of importance be sent him. During the evening a courier brought word from General Wright saying that all was quiet, and that he had ordered a strong reconnoissance to go and develop the enemy's position. So we all went to bed without any thought of what awaited us.

In the morning, about daylight, word was brought from the picket-line south of Winchester of heavy firing at the front. General Sheridan interviewed the officer who brought the information, and decided that it must be the result of the reconnoissance that General Wright had notified him the night before was to take place this morning. Little apprehension was occasioned by the report. After breakfast, probably nearly or quite nine o'clock, we mounted and rode at a walk through the town of Winchester to Mill Creek, a mile south of the village, where we found our escort awaiting us.

We could occasionally hear the far-away sound of heavy guns, and as we moved out with our escort behind us I thought that the general was becoming anxious. He leaned forward and listened intently, and once he dismounted and placed his ear near the ground, seeming somewhat disconcerted as he rose again and remounted. We had not gone far, probably not more than a mile, when, at the crest of a little hill on the road, we found the pike obstructed by some supply-trains which had started on their way to the army. They were now halted, and seemingly in great confusion. Part of the wagons faced one way, part the other; others were half turned round, in position to swing either way, but were huddled together, completely blocking the road.

Turning to me, the general said, " Ride forward quickly and find out the trouble here, and report promptly." I rode rapidly to the head of the train and asked for the quartermaster in charge, and was told he had gone up the road a short distance.

On reaching him, I found him conversing with a quartermaster-sergeant. They informed me that an officer had come from the front and told them to go back at once, as our army had been attacked at daylight, defeated, and was being driven down the valley. The officer, they said, had gone back towards the front after warning them to come no further.

Galloping back, I made my report. " Pick out fifty of the best-mounted men from the escort," was the response. Riding down the column, with the aid of one of the officers of the regiment, this was soon accomplished, and I reported with the selected men. Turning to his chief of staff, Colonel J. W. Forsyth, the general said something regarding certain instructions he had evidently been giving him, and then said to me, " You and Captain O'Keeffe will go with me;" and nodding good-bye to the other gentlemen of our party, with whom he had probably been conferring while I was making up the cavalry detail, he turned his horse's head southward, tightening the reins of his bridle, and with a slight touch of the spur he dashed up the turnpike and was off. A yard in rear, and side by side, Captain O'Keeffe and myself swept after him, while the escort, breaking from a trot to a gallop, came thundering on behind.

The distance from Winchester to Cedar Creek, on the north bank of which the Army of the Shenandoah lay encamped, is a little less than nineteen miles. The general direction was west of south, and the road to it, by way of the valley pike, ran directly through the road-side hamlets of Milltown, Kearnstown, Newtown, and Middletown. Our army was encamped four miles south of Middletown. The Shenandoah Valley turnpike, over which we were now speeding, was formerly a well-built macadamized road, laid in crushed limestone, and until the advent of the war had been kept in excellent condition. Even now, though worn for three years past by the tread of contending armies with all the paraphernalia of war as they swept up and down the valley, it was a fairly good road; but the army supply - trains, ammunition - wagons, and artillery had worn it into deep ruts in places, and everywhere the dust lay thick and heavy on its surface, and powdered the trees and bushes that fringed its sides, so that our galloping column sent a gray cloud swirling behind us. It was a golden sunny day that had succeeded a densely foggy October morning. The turnpike stretched away, a white, dusty line, over hill and through dale, bordered by fenceless fields, and past farm-houses and empty barns and straggling orchards. Now and then it ran through a woody copse, with here and there a tiny stream of water crossing it, or meandering by its side, so clear and limpid that it seemed to invite us to pause and slake our thirst as we sped along our dusty way. On either side we saw, through the Indian-summer haze, the distant hills covered with woods and fairly ablaze with foliage; and over all was the deep blue of a cloudless Southern sky, making it a day on which one's blood ran riot and he was glad of health and life.

Within a mile we met more supply-trains that had turned back, and the general stopped long enough to order the officer in charge to halt, park his trains just where he was, and await further instructions. Then on we dashed again, only to meet, within a few moments, more supply-trains hurrying to the rear. The general did not stop, but signalling the officer in charge to join him, gave him instructions on the gallop to park his train at once, and use his escort to arrest and stop all stragglers coming from the army, and to send back to the front all well men who might drift to him, under guard if necessary.

Scarcely had we parted from him and surmounted the next rise in the road when we came suddenly upon indubitable evidence of battle and retreat. About a mile in advance of us the road was filled and the fields dotted with wagons and men belonging to the various brigade, division, and corps headquarters, and in among them officers' servants with led horses, and here and there a broken ambulance, sutlers' supply-trains, a battery forge or two, horses and mules hastily packed with officers' mess kits, led by their cooks, and now and then a group of soldiers, evidently detailed enlisted men attached to the headquarters trains. In fact, this was the first driftwood of a flood just beyond and soon to come sweeping down the road. Passing this accumulation of débris with a rush by leaving the pike and galloping over the open fields on the side of the road, we pushed rapidly on ; but not so quickly but that we caught an echoing cheer from the enlisted men and servants, who recognized the general, and shouted and swung their hats in glee.

Within the next few miles the pike and adjacent fields began to be lined and dotted everywhere with army wagons, sutlers' outfits, headquarters supply - trains, disabled caissons, and teamsters with led mules, all drifting to the rear ; and now and then a wounded officer or enlisted man on horseback or plodding along on foot, with groups of straggling soldiers here and there among the wagon-trains, or in the fields, or sometimes sitting or lying down to rest by the side of the road, while others were making coffee

in their tin cups by tiny camp-fires. Soon we began to see small bodies of soldiers in the fields
with stacked arms, evidently cooking breakfast.
As we debouched into the fields and passed around
the wagons and through these groups, the general would wave his hat to the men and point to the
front, never lessening his speed as he pressed forward. It was enough; one glance at the eager
face and familiar black horse and they knew him,
and starting to their feet, they swung their caps
around their heads and broke into cheers as he
passed beyond them; and then, gathering up
their belongings and shouldering their arms,
they started after him for the front, shouting to
their comrades further out in the fields, " Sheridan! Sheridan!" waving their hats, and pointing
after him as he dashed onward; and they too
comprehended instantly, for they took up the
cheer and turned back for the battle-field.

To the best of my recollection, from the time
we met the first stragglers who had drifted back
from the army, his appearance and his cheery
shout of " Turn back, men! turn back! Face
the other way!" as he waved his hat towards the
front, had but one result: a wild cheer of recognition, an answering wave of the cap. In no
case, as I glanced back, did I fail to see the men
shoulder their arms and follow us. I think it is
no exaggeration to say that as he dashed on to

the field of battle, for miles back the turnpike was lined with men pressing forward after him to the front.

So rapid had been our gait that nearly all of the escort, save the commanding officer and a few of his best-mounted men, had been distanced, for they were more heavily weighted, and ordinary troop horses could not live at such a pace. Once we were safe among our own people, their commander had the good sense to see that his services were no longer a necessity, and accordingly drew rein and saved his horses by following on at a slow trot. Once the general halted a moment to speak to an officer he knew and inquire for information. As he did so he turned and asked me to get him a switch; for he usually rode carrying a light riding-whip, and furthermore he had broken one of the rowels of his spurs. Dismounting, I cut one from a near-by way-side bush, hastily trimmed it, and gave it him. " Thanks, Sandy," said he, and as we started again he struck his splendid black charger Rienzi a slight blow across the shoulder with it, and he at once broke into that long swinging gallop, almost a run, which he seemed to maintain so easily and so endlessly—a most distressing gait for those who had to follow far. These two words of thanks were nearly the only ones he addressed to me until we reached the army; but my eyes had sought his face at every opportunity, and my heart beat high with hope from what I saw there. As he galloped on his features gradually grew set, as though carved in stone, and the same dull red glint I had seen in his piercing black eyes when, on other occasions, the battle was going against us, was there now. Occasionally Captain O'Keeffe and myself exchanged a few words, and we waved our hats and shouted to the men on the road and in the fields as we passed them, pointing to the general and seconding as best we could his energetic shout: " Turn back, men! turn back! Face the other way!" Now and then I would glance at the face of my companion, Captain O'Keeffe, whose gray-blue eyes fairly danced with excitement at the prospect of the coming fray; for if ever a man was a born soldier and loved fighting for chivalry's sake, it was that gallant young Irish gentleman, Joe O'Keeffe.*

Each moment that we advanced the road became more closely clogged with stragglers and wounded men, and here the general suddenly

* Captain O'Keeffe had been a soldier in the Pope's guard, and was, I think, a relative of the Bishop of Cork. He came to this country, tendering his sword to the government, and was made an aide-de-camp. He resigned this position to become Major of the Second New York Cavalry, and was mortally wounded at the battle of Five Forks, April 1, 1865.

paused to speak to one of the wounded officers,
from whom I judge he got his only correct idea
of the attack by the enemy at dawn, the crush-
ing of our left, and the steady outflanking that
had forced our army back to where it was at
present, for I caught something of what the officer said, and his ideas seemed to be clear and
concise. This pause was a piece of rare good
fortune for me, for my orderly happened to be by
the side of the road with my led horse, and in a
trice he changed my saddle, and I rejoined the
general ere he was a hundred yards away, with
all the elation that a fresh mount after a weary
one inspires in the heart of a cavalryman.

Within a comparatively short distance we
came suddenly upon a field-hospital in a farm-
house close to the road beyond Newtown, where
the medical director had established part of his
corps. Just ahead of us the road was filled with
ambulances containing wounded men, who were
being carried into the house to be operated upon,
while outside of the door along the foot-path lay
several dead men, who had been hastily placed
there on being taken from the stretchers. The
vicinity was dotted with wounded men, sitting
or lying down or standing around, waiting to
have their wounds dressed, while the surgeons
were flitting here and there doing their best and
straining every nerve to meet their necessities.

Giving the place a wide berth, after the first glance, and galloping around the line of ambulances that filled the pike, we passed through a fringe of woods, up a slight eminence in the road, and in a flash we were in full view of the battle-field. It was a grewsome sight to meet the eyes of a commanding general who, three short days before, had left it a triumphant host lying quietly in camp, resting securely on its victories, and confident in its own strength. And now!

In our immediate front the road and adjacent fields were filled with sections of artillery, caissons, ammunition - trains, ambulances, battery-wagons, squads of mounted men, led horses, wounded soldiers, broken wagons, stragglers, and stretcher - bearers—in fact, all that appertains to and is part of the rear of an army in action. One hasty glance as we galloped forward and we had taken in the situation. About half or three-quarters of a mile this side of Middletown, with its left resting upon the turnpike, was a division of infantry in line of battle at right angles to the road, with its standards flying, and evidently held well in hand. Near the turnpike, and just to its left, one of our batteries was having a savage artillery duel with a Confederate battery, which was in position on a little hill to the left and rear of Middletown as we faced it. To the left of this battery of ours were the led horses of a small brigade of cavalry, which was holding the ground to the left of the pike, and both the infantry and cavalry dismounted skirmishers were in action with those of the enemy. Further to the left, and slightly to the rear, on a bit of rising ground, was another of our batteries in action. Half a mile to the right, and somewhat to the rear of the division of infantry which was in line of battle, could be seen a body of infantry in column slowly retiring and tending towards the pike; and just beyond these troops was another body of infantry, also in column, and also moving in the same general direction. Further to the right, across a small valley, and more than a mile away from these last-mentioned troops, was a still larger force of infantry, on a side-hill, facing towards the enemy, in line of battle, but not in action. I looked in vain for the cavalry divisions, but concluded rightly that they were somewhere on the flanks of the enemy.

Skirting the road, and avoiding as best we might the impedimenta of battle, the general, O'Keeffe, and myself spurred forward. Finally, on the open road and just before we reached the troops in line, which was Getty's division of the Sixth Army Corps, I asked permission to go directly down to the skirmish-line to see the actual

" ' SHERIDAN !   SHERIDAN !' "

condition of things. " Do so," replied the general, " and report as soon as possible." Just then we reached the line, and as I glanced back I saw the chief draw rein in the midst of the division, where he was greeted by a storm of cheers and wild cries of "Sheridan! Sheridan!" while standards seemed to spring up out of the very earth to greet him. A few seconds later and I was on the skirmish-line by the side of Colonel Charles R. Lowell, commanding the regular cavalry brigade.

" Is Sheridan here?"

" Yes."

" Thank goodness for that!"

At this moment Mr. Stillson, the war correspondent of one 'of the New York newspapers (who had risked his life for news more than once, and in fact was doing it now), rode up and made the same inquiry.

" He is here," was my reply.

" Well? What is he going to do about it?"

" He's going to whale blank out of them."

" He can't do it," shaking his head.

" Wait, and you'll see."

" I wish I may," said the plucky correspondent, " but I doubt it," and he turned and rode back to find the general.

Turning again to Colonel Lowell, I eagerly asked for the facts about the battle, well knowing that there was no cooler head or better brain in all the army, nor one to be more absolutely relied upon. As we rode along the skirmish-line, that I might get a better view of the enemy, he gave me the details as he knew them. Then, as we watched the enemy forming his battalions in the distance for another advance, I put the question:

" Can you hold on here forty minutes?"

" Yes."

" Can you make it sixty?"

" It depends; you see what they are doing. I will if I can."

" Hold on as long as possible," said I; and turning, I rode rapidly back to my chief, whom I found dismounted, surrounded by several general officers, and in the midst of those of his staff who had not gone with us to Washington. Dismounting, I saluted. Stepping on one side from the group, he faced me, and said,

" Well?"

" You see where we are?" (A nod.) " Lowell says that our losses, killed, wounded, and missing, are between three and five thousand, and more than twenty guns, to say nothing of transportation. He thinks he can hold on where he is for forty minutes longer, possibly sixty."

I can see him before me now as I write, erect, looking intently in my eyes, his left hand resting, clinched savagely, on the top of the hilt of his sabre, his right nervously stroking his chin, his eyes with that strange red gleam in them, and his attenuated features set as if cast in bronze. He stood mute and absolutely still for more than ten seconds; then, throwing up his head, he said:

"Go to the right and find the other two divisions of the Sixth Corps, and also General Emory's command [the two divisions of the Nineteenth Corps]. Bring them up, and order them to take position on the right of Getty. Lose no time." And as I turned to mount, he called out: "Stay! I'll go with you!" And springing on his horse, we set off together, followed by the staff.

Riding up closely to him, I said, "Pardon me, general, but I think if I had control of a division I could do good work here."

Looking me squarely in the eyes for a few seconds, he replied: "Do you? Perhaps I'll give you control of more than that."

Not another word was said, and in a few moments we had reached the head of the nearest division we were seeking. It was ordered on the line—I think by the general himself; and as I started for the head of the other division, he ordered me to ride directly over to General Emory's command (two divisions of the Nineteenth Corps), and order it up, to take position in line of battle on the right of the Sixth Corps. I rode over to General Emory's line, which was about a mile away, and found his troops in good condition, though somewhat shattered by the fortunes of the day, facing towards the enemy, and half covered by small ledges of rock that cropped out of the hill-side. On receiving the order, he called my attention to the fact that in case the enemy advanced on the Sixth Corps, he would be nearly on their flank, and thought best that I apprise the commanding general of the fact, as it might induce him to modify the order. Galloping back, I gave his suggestion to the general.

" *No, no !* " he replied. " Get him over *at once —at once !* Don't lose a moment!"

I fairly tore back, and the troops were promptly put in motion for their new position, which they reached in due time, and were formed in line of battle in accordance with General Sheridan's orders.*

After the whole line was thoroughly formed, I rode over to my chief and urged him to ride down

---

*I found General Sheridan standing on the line of battle on the pike at the junction of General Getty's division of the Sixth Corps and the remnant of the Army of West Virginia, or what was called the Eighth Corps. In the group of officers who were standing around him were General R. B. Hayes and Lieutenant William McKinley, both of whom have since been President of the United States.

" ' STAY HERE AND HELP ME FIGHT THIS CORPS' "

it, that all the men might see him, and know without doubt that he had returned and assumed command.   At first he demurred, but I was most urgent, as I knew that in some instances both men and officers who had not seen him doubted his arrival.   His appearance was greeted by tremendous cheers from one end of the line to the other, many of the officers pressing forward to shake his hand.   He spoke to them all, cheerily and confidently, saying: " We are going back to our camps, men, never fear.   I'll get a twist on these people yet.   We'll raise them out of their boots before the day is over."

At no time did I hear him utter that " terrible oath " so often alluded to in both prose and poetry in connection with this day's work.

As we turned to go back from the end of the line, he halted on the line of the Nineteenth Corps and said to me: " Stay here and help fight this corps.   I will send orders to General Emory through you.   Give orders in my name, if necessary.   Stay right on this line with it."

" Very good, general," was my reply; and the general and staff left me there and galloped towards the pike.

It must have been nearly or quite half-past twelve o'clock by this time, and as soon as the skirmishers were thrown forward the troops were ordered to lie down; an order gladly obeyed, for they had been on their feet since daylight, fighting and without food. They were to have but a short period of rest, however, for in a few moments the low rustling murmur, that presages the advance of a line of battle through dense woods (the Nineteenth Corps was formed just at the outer edge of a belt of heavy timber) began to make itself felt, and in a moment the men were in line again. A pattering fire in front, and our skirmishers came quickly back through the woods, and were absorbed in the line; then there was a momentary lull, followed by a rustling, crunching sound as the enemy's line pressed forward, trampling the bushes under foot, and crowding through bits of underbrush.

In a flash we caught a glimpse of a long gray line stretching away through the woods on either side of us, advancing with waving standards, with here and there a mounted officer in rear of it. At the same instant the dark blue line at the edge of the woods seemed to burst upon their view, for suddenly they halted, and with a piercing yell poured in a heavy volley, that was almost instantly answered from our side, and then volleys seemed fairly to leap from one end to the other of our line, and a steady roar of musketry from both sides made the woods echo again in every direction. Gradually, however, the sounds became less heavy and intense, the volleys slowly

died away, and we began to recognize the fact
that the enemy's bullets were no longer clipping
the twigs above us, and that their fire had about
ceased, while a ringing cheer along our front
proclaimed that for the first time that day the
Confederate army had been repulsed.

During the attack my whole thought, and I
believe that of every officer on the line, had been
to prevent our troops from giving way. In one
or two places the line wavered slightly, but the
universal shout of "Steady, men, *steady, steady!*"
as the field-officers rode up and down the line,
seemed to be all that was needed to inspire the
few nervous ones with renewed courage and hold
them well up to their work. As for myself, I
was more than satisfied, for only years of personal experience in war enable a man to appreciate at its actual value the tremendous gain
when a routed army turns, faces, and checks a
triumphant enemy in the open field. It is a great
thing to do it with the aid of reinforcements; it
is a glorious thing to do it without.

For a few moments the men stood leaning on
their arms, and some of us mounted officers rode
slowly forward, anxiously peering through the
trees, but save for a dead man or two there was
no sign of the enemy; the Confederates had fallen
back. Word was passed back to the line, and the
men were ordered to lie down, which they willing-

ly did.   I rode slowly up and down the line of the
Nineteenth Corps, and after a few moments grew
impatient for orders, for as a cavalryman my
first thought, after the repulse of the enemy, was
a countercharge.   The minutes crept slowly by,
and nothing came, not even an aide for information.   Twenty minutes elapsed, thirty, forty,
fifty, and I could wait no longer, but galloped
to army headquarters, which I found to the right
of the turnpike, about two hundred yards in rear
of the Sixth Corps.   Dismounting, I went up and
saluted the commanding general, who was half
lying down, with his head resting on his right
hand, his elbow on the ground, and surrounded
by most of his staff.   Colonel J. W. Forsyth, his
chief of staff, as well as Colonels Alexander and
Thom of the Engineer Corps, were with him, having reached the field since I had been on the line
with the Nineteenth Corps.

"Well, what is it?" said the general.

"It seems to me, general, that we ought to advance; I have come hoping for orders." He half
sat up, and the black eyes flashed.   I realized
that I had laid myself open to censure; but gradually an amused look overshadowed the anxious
face, and the chief slowly shook his head.

"Not yet, not yet; go back and wait."

I saluted, mounted, and rode leisurely back,
cogitating as I went.   I knew that there must

be some good reason for the delay, but as yet I was unable to fathom it. Reaching the rear of the centre of the Nineteenth Corps, I found a shady spot, and dismounting, sat down on the ground just back of the line, holding my horse's bridle in my hand, for I had no orderly with me. Very soon I became interested in watching the various phases of the situation as they developed before me, and I soon saw one reason for delay, and that was that we were steadily growing stronger. The tired troops had thrown themselves on the ground at the edge of the woods, and lay on their arms in line of battle, listlessly and sleepily. Every now and then stragglers— sometimes singly, oftener in groups—came up from the rear, and moving along back of the line, dusty, heavy-footed, and tired, found and rejoined their respective companies and regiments, dropping down quietly by the side of their companions as they came to them, with a gibe or a word or two of greeting on either side, and then they, too, like most of the rest, subsided into an appearance of apathetic indifference. Here and there men loaded with canteens were sent to the rear in search of water; and every few yards soldiers lay munching a bit of hardtack, the first food many of them had had during the day, for they were driven from their camps at daylight.

Little was said by officers or men, for the truth

was that nearly all were tired, troubled, and somewhat disheartened by the disaster that had so unexpectedly overtaken them; for even in the light of existing events the Confederates had triumphed. They had been routed from their position, their left overwhelmed, crushed, and driven in upon the centre, and the whole army repeatedly outflanked and forced back beyond Middletown, a distance of nearly five miles, where they now were, with the loss of many cannon, most of their wounded, thousands of prisoners, and quantities of transportation—this, too, by a foe whom they believed practically vanquished, and whom they had defeated in pitched battle twice within the last thirty days. This unpalatable fact burned itself into their brain as they lay prone on the ground, with their rifles beside them, trying to snatch a few moments' troubled sleep for their heavy eyes and weary bodies. It must have been a bitter cud to chew.

As the moments continued to pass with no orders from headquarters I grew impatient again, notwithstanding the fact that the delay was increasing our strength by the return of stragglers and the reorganization of scattered regiments, as well as giving a much-needed rest to the whole army. For the foe was also resting, and probably gaining strength in the same manner, so I mounted and passed through our line, and rode

out towards the enemy as far as I could with reasonable safety. Owing to the woods and the
conformation of the ground, I could not accurate-
ly determine anything, so I came back and went
again to army headquarters. I reported my actions, and told the general how I had not been
able to satisfy myself as to the present location
of the enemy's line, but I thought the men were
sufficiently rested to advance in good heart. He
did not reply immediately, but seemed thoughtful
and perplexed.

Finally he shook his head, and said, " Not yet,
not yet; go back and wait patiently."

Riding back to my former location, I dismounted and sat down again, much puzzled to know
the reason for this inaction, as it was so unlike
what I had seen of my chief, who was always so
quick to see and prompt to act, especially on the
field of battle. I think it must have been nearly
an hour when I again passed to the front of our
line, gave my horse to one of the skirmishers, and
cautiously stole through the woods, till, on sur-
mounting a slight rise, I distinctly heard sounds
that indicated the vicinity of the enemy, and by
crawling forward I saw his line in the distance,
and made out that the Confederates were piling
up stones and rails on the prolongation of a line
of stone fences, evidently expecting an advance
from our side and preparing for it.

I returned at once, and for the third time reported at army headquarters. As I came up I noticed that the general had evidently just received a report of some kind from an officer who was riding off as I made my appearance. Reporting what I had heard and seen, he glanced up brightly and said:

"It's all right now! I have been kept back by a report of troops coming down in our rear by way of the Front Royal pike. It's not so, however." Then, turning to one of his staff officers, he asked for the time of day.

" Twenty minutes to four," was the reply.

"So late!" said the general. "Why, that's later than I thought!" And then, turning again to me, he said: "Tell General Wright to move forward the Sixth Corps and attack at once, keeping his left on the pike; then tell General Emory to advance at the same time, keeping the left of the Nineteenth Corps well closed on the right of the Sixth Corps; if opportunity offers, swing the right division of the Nineteenth Corps to the left, and drive the enemy towards the pike. I will put what is available of General Crook's forces on the left of the pike and General Merritt's cavalry also, and send Custer well out on Emory's right to cover that flank. Do you clearly comprehend?"

"Certainly! The Sixth and Nineteenth Corps

attack, with Merritt's cavalry on the left and Custer's on the right, the right division of the Nineteenth to try and outflank the enemy and swing towards the pike."

"Good!" said the general, with a quick nod, and I saluted and sprang to my saddle with a feeling of elation difficult for one not a soldier to adequately comprehend.

I found General Wright just in rear of his corps, lying on the ground. He sat up as I reported, and I saw that his beard was clotted with blood and his neck and chin swollen, and he spoke with something of an effort. He had been shot just under the chin early in the day, but had retained command of the army until General Sheridan's arrival, and then assumed command of his own corps. On receiving General Sheridan's order, he said:

"Do I understand that General Emory's troops connect with my right flank?"

"Certainly!"

"And General Crook's forces will be on the left of the pike?"

"Yes, and General Merritt's cavalry also."

"Very well."

And as I saluted and turned away he was already giving orders to his aides. I rode rapidly to General Emory and repeated the commanding general's instructions, and then returned to my

former station in rear of the right centre of the
Nineteenth Corps.

In a few moments the news ran down the line
that we were to advance. Springing to their
feet at the word of command, the tired troops
stood to arms and seemed to resolutely shake
off the depression that had sat so heavily upon
them, and began to pull themselves together for
the coming fray. Everywhere along the line
of battle men might be seen to stoop and retie
their shoes; to pull their trousers at the ankle
tightly together and then draw up their heavy
woollen stockings over them; to rebuckle and
tighten their waist-belts; to unbutton the lids
of their cartridge-boxes and pull them forward
rather more to the front; to rearrange their hav-
ersacks and canteens, and to shift their rolls of
blankets in order to give freer scope to the expan-
sion of their shoulders and an easier play to their
arms; to set their forage-caps tighter on their
heads, pulling the vizor well down over their eyes;
and then, almost as if by order, there rang from
one end of the line to the other the rattle of ram-
rods and snapping of gunlocks as each man
tested for himself the condition of his rifle, and
made sure that his weapon was in good order
and to be depended upon in the emergency that
was so soon to arise. Then, grounding arms,
they stood at ease, half leaning on their rifles,

saying little, but quietly awaiting orders and grimly gazing straight towards the front. In front of the battalions, with drawn swords and set lips, stood their line-officers, slightly craning their heads forward and looking into the woods, as if trying to catch a glimpse of the enemy they knew to be somewhere there, but whom as yet they could not see.

I push through the line slightly forward of the nearest brigade, and in a moment the sharp command, "Attention!" rings down the line. "Shoulder arms! Forward! *March!*" And with martial tread and floating flags the line of battle is away. "Guide left!" shout the line-officers. "Guide left—*left!*" and that is the only order I hear as we press forward through the thick trees and underbrush. I lean well forward on my horse's neck, striving to catch if possible a glimpse of the Confederate line; but hark! Here comes the first shot. "Steady! *Steady,* men!" Another, and now a few scattering bullets come singing through the woods. The line does not halt or return the fire, but presses steadily on to the oft-repeated command of "Forward! *forward!*" that never ceases to ring from one end to the other of the advancing line. Soon the woods become less dense, and through the trees I see just beyond us an open field partly covered with small bushes, and several hundred yards away, crowning a slight crest on its further side, a low line of fence-rails and loose stones, which, as we leave the edge of the woods, and come into the open, suddenly vomits flame and smoke along its entire length, and a crashing volley tells us that we have found the enemy. For an instant our line staggers, but the volley has been aimed too high and few men fall. "Steady —steady, men!" shout the officers. "*Aim!*" and almost instinctively the whole line throw forward their pieces. "*Fire!*" and the next instant a savage volley answers that of the Confederates. I can see that it has told, too, for in several places along the opposite crest men spring to their feet as if to fall back, but their officers promptly rally them. "Pour it into them, men!" shout our officers. "Let them have it. It's our turn now!" for brute instinct has triumphed and the savage is uppermost with all of us. For a moment or two the men stand and fire at will, as rapidly as it is possible to reload, and then the Confederate fire seems to slowly slacken; so, with a universal shout of "Forward! *forward!*" we press towards the enemy's line. Before we are much more than half way across the field, however, they seem to have abandoned our front, for I cannot see anything ahead of us, though I stand up in my stirrups and look eagerly forward. But what—what is that? *Crash!*

"'HOLDING ON TO MY SADDLE, THE COLOR-BEARER ACCOMPANIES ME'"

crash ! and from a little bush-covered plateau on our right the enemy sends a couple of rattling volleys on our exposed flank that do us great harm, and I realize that *we are the outflanked !*

For an instant the line gives way, but every mounted officer in the vicinity, among whom I recognize General Fessenden, seems to be instantly on the spot trying to rally the troops and hold the line. *"Steady! steady! Right wheel!"* is the shout, and the men, after the first flush of surprise, behave splendidly, one young color-bearer rushing to the right and waving his flag defiantly in the new direction from which the enemy's fire is now coming. I ask him to let me take it, as I am mounted and it can be seen better, as there is some undergrowth at this particular spot in the field. At first he demurs, but seeing the point, yields. Holding on to my saddle, the color-bearer accompanies me towards a slight hillock. The line catches sight of it, and the left begins to swing slowly round, the men in our immediate vicinity loading and firing as rapidly as they can in the direction from which the enemy is now advancing. The Confederates are giving it to us hot, and we realize that we have lost the continuity of our line on both flanks.

Suddenly peal on peal of musketry broke out on our right, and the copse in front of us was fairly bullet-swept by repeated volleys. The next moment a portion of one of McMillan's brigades, which he had promptly swung round and faced to the right, dashed forward, and together we moved up to the position just held by the enemy, to find that he was in headlong retreat. One hasty look and I saw that we had pierced the enemy's line, and that his extreme left was cut off and scattered. But I could not see any troops nor anything of his line over in the direction of the pike, as there was a dense belt of woods that shut out the view. Nevertheless, the steady roar of artillery and peals of musketry told us that heavy fighting was going on in that part of the field. General McMillan was already re-forming his men to move over and take up the line and our former direction to the left, when General Sheridan, riding his gray charger Breckenridge, and surrounded by his staff, came out of the woods and dashed up. One glance and he had the situation. " This is all right! this is all right!" was his sole comment. Then turning to General McMillan, he directed him to continue the movement and close up to the left and complete our line of battle as it originally was.

He told me, however, to hold the troops until I saw that Custer had driven the enemy's cavalry from our flank. This we could easily see, as the country was open and the ground lower than where we were. Having given these instructions, the general, followed by his staff, galloped rapidly to the left and rear through the woods, evidently making for the pike, where, judging from the continued roar of field-guns and musketry, the Sixth Corps was having savage work.

As soon as we saw General Custer's squadrons charge across the field and engage the enemy's cavalry, General McMillan ordered the advance, and we pushed forward, driving the enemy ahead of us through the wood, and came out to the left and rear of the Confederate line, enabling our left to pour in a fearful fire on their exposed flank. The enemy was gallantly holding his line behind some stone fences, but " flesh that is born of woman " could not stand such work as this, and the cavalry, having got well in on their right flank about this time, their entire line gave way in retreat.

Our whole army now pressed rapidly forward, not stopping to re-form, but driving them from each new line of defence; but it was no walkover even then, for the Confederates fought splendidly—desperately even. They tried to take advantage of every stone fence, house, or piece of woods on which to rally their men and retard our advance. Their batteries were served gallantly and handled brilliantly, and took up position after position; but it was all in vain, for we outnumbered them, both cavalry and infantry, and their men must have comprehended the fact that our cavalry was turning both their flanks. They made their last stand on the hills just this side of Cedar Creek, occupying the reverse side of some of our own earthworks; and when the infantry I was with came up to Belle Plain, which was the house General Sheridan had occupied as headquarters prior to his departure for Washington, it was already getting quite dark. I dismounted here and ran in a moment to see whether Colonel Tolles and Dr. Ohlenschlaeger, two of General Sheridan's staff who had been wounded by guerillas, were still living. They were still alive, but unconscious, and some one (a Confederate, I think), fearing that the house might be shelled during the action, had placed their mattresses on the floor to keep them as far out of harm's way as possible. Hurrying out, I pushed on with the infantry.

For a few moments the Confederates held their position on the hills, but suddenly abandoned it in haste and sought safety in flight, for some of General Custer's cavalry had crossed the creek at the ford below and were getting in their rear, and to remain was to be captured. I soon caught up with some of our cavalry regiments, and we started in full cry after the enemy. It was no use for them to attempt anything but flight from this on, and they abandoned everything and got away from our pursuing squadrons as best they might, hundreds of them leaving the pike and scattering through the hills. On we went, pell-mell, in the dark. Two regiments, the Fifth New York Cavalry and the First Vermont Cavalry, to the best of my recollection, were the only regimental organizations that went beyond Strasburg. The road was literally crammed with abandoned wagons, ambulances, caissons, and artillery.

At a small bridge, where a creek crosses the road some distance south of the town, we were fired upon from the opposite side by what I thought was the last organized force of General Early's army. I now believe it to have been his provost guard with a large body of our prisoners captured by the enemy early in the day. The planks of this bridge were torn up to prevent the enemy from coming back during the night and carrying off any of the captured property. I then started to return to headquarters, counting the captured cannon as I went. It soon occurred to me that as it was so dark I might mistake a caisson for a gun, so I dismounted and placed my hand on each piece. I reached headquarters about half-past eight or possibly nine o'clock. Camp-fires were blazing everywhere. I went up to the chief, who was standing near a bright fire surrounded by a group of officers. and saluted, reporting my return.

" Where do you come from?"

" Beyond Strasburg."

" What news have you?"

" The road is lined with transportation of almost every kind, and we have captured forty-four pieces of artillery."

" How do you *know* that we have forty-four pieces?"

" I have placed my hand on each and every gun."

Standing there in the firelight I saw my chief's face light up with a great wave of satisfaction.

THE CLOSING SCENE AT APPO-MATTOX COURT-HOUSE

THE CLOSING SCENE AT APPO-
MATTOX COURT-HOUSE

WHEN, on the night of the 8th of April, 1865,
the cavalry corps of the Army of the Potomac reached the two or three little houses that
made up the settlement at Appomattox Depot—
the station on the South-side Railroad that con-
nects Appomattox Court-house with the travel-
ling world—it must have been nearly or quite
dark. At about nine o'clock or half-past, while
standing near the door of one of the houses, it
occurred to me that it might be well to try and get
a clearer idea of our immediate surroundings,
as it was not impossible that we might have hot
work here or near here before the next day fairly
dawned upon us.

My " striker " had just left me with instructions to have my horse fed, groomed, and saddled
before daylight. As he turned to go he paused
and put this question: " Do you think, Colonel,
that we'll get General Lee's army to-morrow?"

" I don't know," was my reply; " but we will have some savage fighting if we don't."

As the sturdy young soldier said " Good-night, sir," and walked away, I knew that if the enlisted men of our army could forecast the coming of the end so plainly, there was little hope of the escape of the Army of Northern Virginia.

I walked up the road a short distance, and looked carefully about me to take my bearings. It was a mild spring night, with a cloudy sky, and the soft mellow smell of earthiness in the atmosphere that not infrequently portends rain. If rain came then it might retard the arrival of our infantry, which I knew General Sheridan was most anxious should reach us at the earliest possible moment. A short distance from where I stood was the encampment of our headquarters escort, with its orderlies, grooms, officers' servants, and horses. Just beyond it could be seen the dying camp-fires of a cavalry regiment, lying close in to cavalry corps headquarters. This regiment was in charge of between six and eight hundred prisoners, who had fallen into our hands just at dark, as Generals Custer and Devin, at the head of their respective cavalry commands, had charged into the station and captured four railway trains of commissariat supplies, which had been sent here to await the arrival of the Confederate army, together with twenty-six pieces of artillery. For a few moments the artillery had greatly surprised and astonished us, for its presence was entirely unexpected, and as it suddenly opened on the charging columns of cavalry it looked for a short time as though we might have all unwittingly fallen upon a division of infantry. However, it turned out otherwise. Our cavalry, after the first recoil, boldly charged in among the batteries, and the gunners, being without adequate support, sensibly surrendered. The whole affair was for us a most gratifying termination of a long day's ride, as it must have proved later on a bitter disappointment to the weary and hungry Confederates pressing forward from Petersburg and Richmond in the vain hope of escape from the Federal troops, who were straining every nerve to overtake them and compel a surrender. To-night the cavalry corps was in their front and squarely across the road to Lynchburg, and it was reasonably certain, should our infantry get up in time on the morrow, that the almost ceaseless marching and fighting of the last ten days were to attain their legitimate result in the capitulation of General Lee's army.

As I stood there in the dark thinking over the work of the twelve preceding days, it was borne in upon me with startling emphasis that to-morrow's sun would rise big with the fate of the

Southern Confederacy; and as I began to recall
the occurrences that had taken place since the
30th of March, I realized for the first time what
a splendid burst it had been for the cavalry corps.
Its superb fighting on the 30th and 31st of March,
at the battle of Dinwiddie Court-house, which
had been the immediate precursor of the great
victory of the battle of Five Forks, won by it
and the Fifth Army Corps on the next day, had
not only crushed the right of the Confederate
line and given us thousands of prisoners, but
had also turned the flank of the Army of Northern
Virginia. This had rendered its vast line of
intrenchments utterly untenable, and, by compelling the retreat of the Confederate army from
before its capital, which it had defended so long
and so successfully, had forced the evacuation
of Petersburg and Richmond. The cavalry
corps had then immediately taken up the pursuit. The Confederate army, once out of its
intrenchments and away from its hoped-for
junction with General Joe Johnston's forces,
and knowing that the Army of the Potomac and
the Army of the James were in full cry in pursuit of it, had time and again turned and fought
gallantly, desperately even, against odds too
great for successful defence, and against troops
better equipped, better fed, and of equal gallantry
in every respect, and, what is more, against men

who knew that the capture of the Army of Northern Virginia meant the close of the war, the end of the great rebellion, the dawn of peace, and their return to their homes, their families, and their firesides.

Scarcely had word reached us of the evacuation of Petersburg and Richmond when, without a second glance at the map, General Sheridan concluded that Danville, on the southern border of the State, was General Lee's objective point, and determined at whatever cost, if within his power, that neither he nor his army should reach it. Probably no man in either army was so well fitted by nature and training to prevent this, if surpassing ability to handle cavalry, an almost intuitive knowledge of topography, a physique that was tireless, dogged tenacity, tremendous energy, and a courage that nothing could daunt, could bring about the desired result. Quick to see and prompt to act, his decision as to the method to be pursued by the cavalry corps was immediate and simple. It was to pursue and attack the left flank of the retreating army at any possible point with the cavalry division that first reached it, and, if possible, compel it to turn and defend its wagon trains and its artillery, then to send another division beyond, and attack the Confederate army again at any other assailable point, and to follow up this method of attack until at some point the whole army would be obliged to turn and deliver battle in the open field to its old opponent, the Army of the Potomac. In vain had General Lee's worn and tired-out cavalry tried to cover his line of retreat and protect his trains, for we were stronger in numbers, far better mounted, and, with no reflection upon our opponents, in a much better state of drill and discipline. Moreover, we had the *élan* of victory and the hope of success, while each succeeding hour they saw their numbers lessening and their hopes fading. Gallant men they were, and, considering the circumstances, bravely and well they fought; but victory for them, with their half-starved men and worn-out horses, was no longer possible.

From the morning of the 2d of April, when General Merritt, with the first cavalry division, caught up with the retreating enemy on the Namozine road, near Scotts Corners, we had given them little or no rest. At Greathouse Creek on the 3d, at Tabernacle Church and Amelia Courthouse on the 4th, at Fames Cross Roads on the 5th, and when brought to bay at Sailor's Creek on the 6th of April, a portion of their army, under General Ewell, halted and gave battle to the cavalry corps and two divisions of the Sixth Army Corps, despite their splendid and desperate fighting, nearly eight thou-

FIGHTING AGAINST FATE

sand of their men, with much of their artillery, were compelled to surrender. The cavalry had given them no rest whatever, and right on their heels came our infantry, constantly attacking and assailing them whenever and wherever they could overtake them. Still they kept plodding wearily on, weak and hungry as they were, holding themselves well together, and turning and fighting bravely where and how they could, but with ever-failing fortune and steadily diminishing numbers, and already many of us, besides General Grant, thought that it was asking too much of these gallant lads in gray to risk their lives longer in support of a confederacy that was tottering to its fall.

General Lee evidently thought otherwise. The next day, the 7th of April, after another fight with the cavalry, at Farmville, he abandoned the idea of reaching Danville, and swinging his retreating army north, from towards the Richmond, Prince Edward, and Danville pike, which had evidently been his objective point, he shaped his course for Lynchburg, Va., over the old Lynchburg and Richmond road. The keen perception of General Sheridan had been but a few hours at fault. Realizing that the Confederate general would probably send for supplies to meet his hungry army at some railway station on the road to Lynchburg, near his line of retreat, he at once decided that Appomattox Depot would be the place, and hurried off his scouts in that direction. The cavalry corps at once abandoned its series of flank attacks on General Lee's retreating army, and pushed out rapidly for that station on the South-side Railroad. Its march led over an old grass-grown dirt road by way of Buffalo River, which ran at times almost parallel with General Lee's retreating army, that was marching south, and for the same objective point, only about twelve or fifteen miles away. General Sheridan's opinion had proved correct, and there we were, the enemy's supplies in our hands, and the cavalry corps squarely across the path of the Confederate army on its way to Lynchburg.

Rapidly as I had thought over the campaign, it was later than I realized as I stepped into the little house near the depot at which General Sheridan had made his headquarters for the night. I found my chief stretched at full length on a bench before a bright open fire, wide-awake, and evidently in deep thought. At that time he was thirty-three years of age, with a clean-cut face, high cheek-bones, fine black eyes, an aggressive chin, slightly aquiline nose, firmly set mouth, dark brown mustache, and close-cut black hair, short in stature—being about five feet four in height, very slight, but wiry and muscular, with a tremendous breadth of shoulder, and long, powerful arms, long-bodied, too, but with very short legs. He sat tall, though, so that when he was mounted he gave one the impression of being quite the average height.

Turning to the chief of staff, Colonel J. W. Forsyth, I said that if there was nothing for me to do I would turn in. He advised me to do so at once, and I accordingly sought my blankets, in the belief that the next day would be a memorable one, either in the way of a desperate engagement between the Confederate army and our cavalry corps (which was at this time, including the horse-artillery and General Mackenzie's cavalry of the Army of the James, about nine thousand strong), or possibly a general engagement between the two armies, in which case I thought there was no hope for the Confederates.

Just before daylight on the morning of the 9th of April I sat down to a cup of coffee, but had hardly begun to drink it when I heard the ominous sound of a scattering skirmish fire, apparently in the direction of Appomattox Court-house. Hastily swallowing what remained of it, I reported to General Sheridan, who directed me to go to the front at once. Springing into the saddle, I galloped up the road, my heart being greatly lightened by a glimpse of two or three infantrymen standing near a camp-fire close by the depot—convincing proof that our hoped-for reinforcements were within supporting distance.

It was barely daylight as I sped along, but before I reached the cavalry brigade of Colonel C. H. Smith that held the main road between Appomattox Court-house and Lynchburg, a distance of about two miles northeast from Appomattox Depot, the enemy had advanced to the attack, and the battle had opened. When ordered into position late the preceding night, Colonel Smith had felt his way in the dark as closely as possible to Appomattox Court-house, and at or near midnight had halted on a ridge, on which he had thrown up a breastwork of rails. This he occupied by dismounting his brigade, and also with a section of horse-artillery, at the same time protecting both his flanks by a small mounted force. As the enemy advanced to the attack in the dim light of early dawn he could not see the led horses of our cavalry, which had been sent well to the rear, and was evidently at a loss to determine what was in his front. The result was that after the first attack he fell back to get his artillery in position, and to form a strong assaulting column against what must have seemed to him a line of infantry. This was most fortunate for us, for by the time he again advanced in full force, and compelled the dismounted cavalry to slowly fall back by weight of numbers, our infantry was hurrying forward from Appomattox Depot (which place it had reached at four o'clock in the morning), and we had gained many precious minutes. At this time most of our cavalry was fighting dismounted, stubbornly retiring. But the Confederates at last realized that there was nothing but a brigade of dismounted cavalry and a few batteries of horse-artillery in their immediate front, and pushed forward grimly and determinedly, driving the dismounted troopers slowly ahead of them.

I had gone to the left of the road, and was in a piece of woods with some of our cavalrymen (who by this time had been ordered to fall back to their horses and give place to our infantry, which was then coming up), when a couple of rounds of canister tore through the branches just over my head. Riding back to the edge of the woods in the direction from which the shots came, I found myself within long pistol range of a section of a battery of light artillery. It was in position near a country road that came out of another piece of woods about two hundred yards in its rear, and was pouring a rapid fire into the woods from which I had just emerged. As I sat on my horse quietly watching it from behind a rail fence, the lieutenant commanding the pieces saw me, and riding out for a hundred yards or more towards where I was, proceeded to cover me with his revolver. We fired together—a miss on both sides. The second shot was uncomfortably close, so far as I was concerned, but as I took deliberate aim for the third shot I became aware that in some way his pistol was disabled; for using both hands and all his strength I saw that he could not cock it. I had him covered, and had he turned I think I should have fired. He did nothing of the sort. Apparently accepting his fate, he laid his revolver across the pommel of his saddle, fronted me quietly and coolly, and looked me steadily in the face. The whole thing had been something in the nature of a duel, and I felt that to fire under the circumstances savored too much of murder. Besides, I knew that at a word from him the guns would have been trained on me where I sat. He, too, seemed to appreciate the fact that it was an individual fight, and manfully and gallantly forbore to call for aid; so lowering and uncocking my pistol, I replaced it in my holster, and shook my fist at him, which action he cordially reciprocated, and then turning away, I rode back into the woods.

Within two hundred yards I met one of our infantry brigades slowly advancing through the trees in line of battle. It was part of the Twenty-fourth Corps of the Army of the James, which had marched nearly all the previous night to

GENEROUS ENEMIES

come to our assistance, and these troops were, I think, the advance of the first division of that corps. I rode up to the commanding officer of these troops and told him where the battery, which was now doing considerable damage among his men, was located, and urged him to dash forward, have the fence thrown down, and charge the guns, which I was sure he could capture. This he refused to do without authority from division or corps headquarters, and while I was eagerly arguing the case, orders came for the line to halt, fall back a short distance, and lie down. I thought then, and do now, that the guns could have been captured with less loss than they finally inflicted on this brigade.

About this time the enemy's artillery ceased firing, and I again rode rapidly to the edge of the woods, just in time to see the guns limber up and retire down the wood road from which they had come. The lieutenant in command saw me and stopped. We simultaneously uncovered, waved our hats to each other, and bowed. I have always thought he was one of the bravest men I ever faced.

I rode back again, passing through our infantry line, intending to go to the left and find the cavalry, which I knew would be on the flank somewhere. Suddenly I became conscious that firing had ceased along the whole line.

I had not ridden more than a hundred yards when I heard some one calling my name. Turning, I saw one of the headquarters aides, who came galloping up, stating that he had been hunting for me for the last fifteen minutes, and that General Sheridan wished me to report to him at once. I followed him rapidly to the right on the wood path in the direction from which he had come.

As soon as I could get abreast of him I asked if he knew what the General wanted me for.

Turning in his saddle, with his eyes fairly ablaze, he said, " Why, don't you know? A white flag."

All I could say was " Really?"

He answered by a nod; and then we leaned towards each other and shook hands; but nothing else was said.

A few moments more and we were out of the woods in the open fields. I saw the long line of battle of the Fifth Army Corps halted, the men standing at rest, the standards being held butt on earth, and the flags floating out languidly on the spring breeze. As we passed them I noticed that the officers had generally grouped themselves in front of the centre of their regiments, sword in hand, and were conversing in low tones. The men were leaning wearily on their rifles, in the position of parade rest. All

THE LAST VICTIM

were anxiously looking to the front, in the direction towards which the enemy's line had withdrawn, for the Confederates had fallen back into a little swale or valley beyond Appomattox Court-house, and were not then visible from this part of our line.

Here and there over the field were small groups of medical officers and stretcher-bearers around a dead or wounded man, showing where the last fire of the skirmishers had taken effect; and as we passed along a portion of the front of the Fifth Corps, I think it was Chamberlin's brigade, we saw just in front of one of the New York regiments a group of sad-eyed officers gathered around the body of one of their number, a fine, stalwart-looking lieutenant, who they told us had been killed by the last shot from the Confederate artillery, just before the order was given to cease firing. He was said to have been a fine officer and a good man, promoted from the ranks for bravery, and it seemed, under the circumstances, a particularly hard fate.

We soon came up to General Sheridan and his staff. They were dismounted, sitting on the grass by the side of a broad country road that led to the Court-house. This was about one or two hundred yards distant, and, as we afterwards found, consisted of the court-house, a small tavern, and eight or ten houses, all situated on this same road or street. Reporting my return, the General quietly acknowledged my salute with a pleasant nod, saying, in reply to my inquiry, that just then he had no immediate need of my services. I saluted, gave my horse to an orderly, and sat down on the grass with the rest of the staff. All nodded smilingly, one or two of my especial friends leaned over and shook hands with me, but not much was said, for we were a tired and thoughtful group.

Conversation was carried on in a low tone, and I was told of the blunder of one of the Confederate regiments in firing on the General and staff after the flag of truce had been accepted. I also heard that General Lee was then up at the little village awaiting the arrival of General Grant, to whom he had sent a note, through General Sheridan, requesting a meeting to arrange terms of surrender. Colonel Newhall, of our headquarters staff, had been despatched in search of General Grant, and might be expected up at almost any moment.

It was, perhaps, something more than an hour and a half later, to the best of my recollection, that General Grant, accompanied by Colonel Newhall, and followed by his staff, came rapidly riding up to where we were standing by the side of the road, for we had all risen at his approach. When within a few yards of us he drew rein, and halted in front of General Sheridan, acknowledged our salute, and then, leaning slightly forward in his saddle, said, in his usual quiet tone, " Good-morning, Sheridan; how are you?"

" First-rate, thank you, General," was the reply. " How are you?"

General Grant nodded in return, and said, " Is General Lee up there?" indicating the Court-house by a glance.

" Yes," was the response, " he's there." And then followed something about the Confederate army, but I did not clearly catch the import of the sentence.

" Very well, then," said General Grant. " Let's go up."

General Sheridan, together with a few selected officers of his staff, mounted, and joined General Grant and staff. Together they rode to Mr. McLean's house, a plain two-story brick residence in the village, to which General Lee had already repaired, and where he was known to be awaiting General Grant's arrival. Dismounting at the gate, the whole party crossed the yard, and the senior officers present went up on to the porch which protected the front of the house. It extended nearly across the entire house and was railed in, except where five or six steps led up the centre opposite the front door, which was flanked by two small wooden benches, placed close against the house on either side of the entrance. The door opened into a hall that ran the entire length of the house, and on either side of it was a single room with a window in each end of it, and two doors, one at the front and one at the rear of each of the rooms, opening on the hall. The room to the left, as you entered, was the parlor, and it was in this room that General Lee was awaiting General Grant's arrival.

As General Grant stepped on to the porch he was met by Colonel Babcock, of his staff, who had in the morning been sent forward with a message to General Lee. He had found him resting at the side of the road, and had accompanied him to McLean's house.*

General Grant went into the house accompanied by General Rawlins, his chief of staff; General Seth Williams, his adjutant-general;

---

* Captain Amos Webster, of General Grant's official staff, was present on this occasion, but informs me that he did not go into the room. Four of the headquarters staff were absent, viz., General C. B. Comstock, who had been sent on a special mission to North Carolina; General F. T. Dent, who was left in charge of field headquarters during General Grant's absence; Captain William McKee Dunn, who had been sent with despatches to General Meade; and Major George K. Leet, A.A.G., who was in Washington. Notwithstanding all the various engravings that have been made of persons who were in the room at Mr. McLean's house at the time of the surrender, I have named all who were actually present in the room at any time during the conference.

General Rufus Ingalls, his quartermaster-general; and his two aides, General Horace Porter and Lieutenant-Colonel Babcock. After a little time General Sheridan; General M. R. Morgan, General Grant's chief commissary; Lieutenant-Colonel Ely Parker, his military secretary; Lieutenant-Colonel T. S. Bowers, one of his assistant adjutants-general; and Captains Robert T. Lincoln and Adam Badeau, aides-de-camp, went into the house at General Grant's express invitation, sent out, I believe, through Colonel Babcock, who came to the hall-door for the purpose, and they were, I was afterwards told, formally presented to General Lee. After a lapse of a few more moments quite a number of these officers, including General Sheridan, came out into the hall and on to the porch, leaving General Grant and General Lee, Generals Rawlins, Ingalls, Seth Williams, and Porter, and Lieutenant-Colonels Babcock, Ely Parker, and Bowers, together with Colonel Marshall, of General Lee's staff, in the room, while the terms of the surrender were finally agreed upon and formally signed. These were the only officers, therefore, who were actually present at the official surrender of the Army of Northern Virginia.

After quite a length of time Colonel Babcock came to the door again, opened it, and glanced out. As he did so he placed his forage-cap on one finger, twirled it around, and nodded to us all, as much as to say, " It's all settled," and said something in a low tone to General Sheridan. Then they, accompanied by General E. O. C. Ord, the commanding general of the Army of the James, who had just ridden up to the house, entered the house together, the hall door being partly closed again after them, leaving quite a number of us staff-officers upon the porch.

While the conference between Generals Grant and Lee was still in progress, Generals Merritt and Custer, of the Cavalry Corps, and several of the infantry generals, together with the rest of General Sheridan's staff-officers, came into the yard, and some of them came up on the porch. Colonel Babcock came out once more, and General Merritt went back to the room with him at his request; but most, if not all, of the infantry generals left us and went back to their respective commands while the conference was still in progress and before it ended.

Just to the right of the house, as we faced it on entering, stood a soldierly looking orderly in a tattered gray uniform, holding three horses— one a fairly well-bred-looking gray, in good heart, though thin in flesh, which, from the accoutrements, I concluded, belonged to General Lee; the others, a thoroughbred bay and a fairly good brown, were undoubtedly those of the staff-officer who had accompanied General Lee, and of the orderly himself. He was evidently a sensible soldier, too, for as he held the bridles he baited the animals on the young grass, and they ate as though they needed all they had a chance to pick up.

I cannot say exactly how long the conference between Generals Grant and Lee lasted, but after quite a while, certainly more than two hours, I became aware from the movement of chairs within that it was about to break up. I had been sitting on the top step of the porch, writing in my field note-book, but I closed it at once, and stepping back on the porch leaned against the railing nearly opposite and to the left of the door, and expectantly waited. As I did so the inner door slowly opened, and General Lee stood before me. As he paused for a few seconds, framed in by the doorway, ere he slowly and deliberately stepped out upon the porch, I took my first and last look at the great Confederate chieftain. This is what I saw: A finely formed man, apparently about sixty years of age, well above the average height, with a clear, ruddy complexion—just then suffused by a deep crimson flush, that rising from his neck overspread his face and even slightly tinged his broad forehead, which, bronzed where it had been exposed to the weather, was clear and beautifully white where it had been shielded by his hat—deep brown eyes, a firm but well-shaped Roman nose, abundant gray hair, silky and fine in texture, with a full gray beard and mustache, neatly trimmed and not over-long, but which, nevertheless, almost completely concealed his mouth. A splendid uniform of Confederate gray cloth, that had evidently seen but little service, was closely buttoned about him, and fitted him to perfection. An exquisitely mounted sword, attached to a gold-embroidered Russia-leather belt, trailed loosely on the floor at his side, and in his right hand he carried a broad-brimmed, soft, gray felt hat, encircled by a golden cord, while in his left he held a pair of buckskin gauntlets. Booted and spurred, still vigorous and erect, he stood bareheaded, looking out of the open doorway, sad-faced and weary: a soldier and a gentleman, bearing himself in defeat with an all-unconscious dignity that sat well upon him.

The moment the open door revealed the Confederate commander, each officer present sprang to his feet, and as General Lee stepped out onto the porch, every hand was raised in military salute. Placing his hat on his head, he mechanically but courteously returned it, and slowly crossed the porch to the head of the steps leading down to the yard, meanwhile keeping his eyes intently fixed in the direction of the little valley over beyond the Court-house, in which his army lay. Here he paused, and slowly drew on his gauntlets, smiting his gloved hands into each other several times after doing so, evidently utterly oblivious of his surroundings. Then, apparently recalling his thoughts, he glanced deliberately right and left, and not seeing his horse, he called, in a hoarse, half-choked voice, " Orderly! Orderly!"

" Here, General, here," was the quick response. The alert young soldier was holding the General's horse near the side of the house. He had taken out the bit, slipped the bridle over the horse's neck, and the wiry gray was eagerly grazing on the fresh young grass about him.

Descending the steps the General passed to the left of the house, and stood in front of his horse's head while he was being bridled. As the orderly was buckling the throat - latch, the General reached up and drew the forelock out from under the brow-band, parted and smoothed it, and then gently patted the gray charger's forehead in an absent-minded way, as one who loves horses, but whose thoughts are far away, might all unwittingly do. Then, as the orderly stepped aside, he caught up the bridle-reins in his left hand, and seizing the pommel of the saddle with the same hand, he caught up the slack of the reins in his right hand, and placing it on the cantle he put his foot in the stirrup, and swung himself slowly and wearily, but nevertheless firmly, into the saddle (the old dragoon mount), letting his right hand rest for an instant or two on the pommel as he settled into his seat, and as he did so there broke unguardedly from his lips a long, low, deep sigh, almost a groan in its intensity, while the flush on his neck and face seemed, if possible, to take on a still deeper hue.

Shortly after General Lee passed down the steps he was followed by an erect, slightly built, soldierly looking officer, in a neat but somewhat worn gray uniform, a man with an anxious and thoughtful face, wearing spectacles, who glanced neither to the right nor left, keeping his eyes straight before him. Notwithstanding this, I doubt if he missed anything within the range of his vision. This officer, I was afterwards told, was Colonel Marshall, one of the Confederate adjutants-general, the member of General Lee's staff whom he had selected to accompany him.

As soon as the Colonel had mounted, General Lee drew up his reins, and, with the Colonel riding on his left, and followed by the orderly, moved at a slow walk across the yard towards the gate.

Just as they started, General Grant came out of the house, crossed the porch, and passed down the steps into the yard. At this time he was nearly forty-two years of age, of middle height, not over-weighted with flesh, but, nevertheless, stockily and sturdily built, light complexion,

DEPARTURE OF GENERAL LEE AFTER THE SURRENDER

mild, gray-blue eyes, finely formed Grecian nose, an iron-willed mouth, brown hair, full brown beard with a tendency toward red rather than black, and in his manner and all his movements there was a strength of purpose, a personal poise, and a cool, quiet air of dignity, decision, and soldierly confidence that were very good to see. On this occasion he wore a plain blue army blouse, with shoulder-straps set with three silver stars equi-distant, designating his rank as Lieutenant-General commanding the armies of the United States; it was unbuttoned, showing a blue military vest, over which and under his blouse was buckled a belt, but he was without a sword. His trousers were dark blue and tucked into top-boots, which were without spurs, but heavily splashed with mud, for once he knew that General Lee was waiting for him at Appomattox Court-house, he had ridden rapidly across country, over road and field and through woods, to meet him. He wore a peculiar stiff-brimmed, sugar-loaf-crowned, campaign hat of black felt, and his uniform was partly covered by a light-weight, dark blue, water-proof, semi-military overcoat, with a full cape, unbuttoned and thrown back, showing the front of his uniform, for while the day had developed into warm, bright, and beautifully sunny weather, the early morning had been damp, slightly foggy, and presaged rain.

As he reached the foot of the steps and started across the yard to the fence, where, inside the gate, the orderlies were holding his horse and those of several of his staff-officers, General Lee, on his way to the gate, rode across his path. Stopping suddenly, General Grant looked up, and both generals simultaneously raised their hands in military salute. After General Lee had passed, General Grant crossed the yard and sprang lightly and quickly into his saddle. He was riding his splendid bay horse Cincinnati, and it would have been difficult to find a firmer seat, a lighter hand, or a better rider in either army.

As he was about to go out of the gate he halted, turned his horse, and rode at a walk towards the porch of the house, where, among others, stood General Sheridan and myself. Stopping in front of the General, he said, " Sheridan, where will you make your headquarters to-night?"

" Here, or near here; right here in this yard, probably," was the reply.

" Very well, then; I'll know where to find you in case I wish to communicate. Good-day."

" Good-day, General," was the response, and with a military salute General Grant turned and rode away.

As he rode forward and halted at the porch to make this inquiry, I had my wished-for opportunity, but my eyes sought his face in vain for

THE MESSAGE OF PEACE

any indication of what was passing in his mind. Whatever may have been there, as Colonel Newhall has well written, " not a muscle of his face told tales on his thoughts "; and if he felt any elation, neither his voice, features, nor his eyes betrayed it. Once out of the gate, General Grant, followed by his staff, turned to the left and moved off at a rapid trot.

General Lee continued on his way towards his army at a walk, to be received by his devoted troops with cheers and tears, and to sit down and pen a farewell order that, to this day, no old soldier of the Army of Northern Virginia can read without moistening eyes and swelling throat.

General Grant, on his way to his field headquarters on this eventful Sunday evening, dismounted, sat quietly down by the road-side, and wrote a short and simple despatch, which a galloping aide bore full speed to the nearest telegraph station, that on its reception in the nation's capital was flashed over the wires to every hamlet in the country, causing every steeple in the North to rock to its foundation, and sent one tall, gaunt, sad-eyed, weary-hearted man in Washington to his knees, thanking God that he had lived to see the beginning of the end, and that he had at last been vouchsafed the assurance that he had led his people aright.

THE END